THE SPIRITUAL CANTICLE
Saint John of the Cross

THE SPIRITUAL CANTICLE

Saint John of the Cross

Modern English Version
with Notes

John Venard OCD

E. J. DWYER

Revised edition published 1990 by
E. J. Dwyer (Australia) Pty Ltd
Unit 3, 32-72 Alice Street
Newtown NSW 2042
Australia
Reprinted 1992

First edition published in 1980

National Library of Australia
Cataloguing-in-Publication data

John, of the Cross, Saint, 1542-1591.
    [Cantico espiritual. English]. The spiritual canticle.
    Modern English version with notes.
    ISBN 0 85574 228 3.

    1. John, of the Cross, Saint, 1542-1591. Cantico
    espiritual. 2. Mystical union. I. Venard, John. II.
    Title.

861.3

Cover designed by Luc Oechslin
Typeset in 10/11 pt Cheltenham by Midland Typesetters, Maryborough
Printed in Singapore by Chong Moh Offset Printing Pte. Ltd

CONTENTS

INTRODUCTION

The Spiritual Canticle of St. John of the Cross was originally a poem of some thirty-one stanzas which he composed when he was imprisoned in Toledo, from December 1577 to August 1578. The Saint drew heavily on the imagery of the Canticle of Canticles, and the early stanzas express something of the desolation of spirit he endured, and his acute sense of the seeming absence of God during the dark days of imprisonment. The rest of the poem, which in its final form numbered forty stanzas, was written at later periods of his life, probably from 1579 to 1583, in Andalusia. In these stanzas something of the fragrant beauty of the countryside in this part of southern Spain comes through, and the whole poem is redolent with the poetic tradition of his native Castile.

The First Redaction of St. John's Commentary on the then thirty-nine stanzas of *The Spiritual Canticle* was set down during 1578–86 in response to the Carmelite nuns' requests for an interpretation of the doctrinal meaning behind the symbolism and imagery. The poem was explained, line by line, usually with an introduction or annotation containing a summary of the Saint's thought on each stanza. The First Redaction was later heavily edited and to a certain extent rewritten by Saint John; Stanza 11 was added, making forty stanzas in all. It is now accepted that both Redactions are authentic. The rearrangement of the stanzas and the many changes in the commentary make for greater clarity and it is the Second Redaction which appears in a simplified version in this book.

The Spiritual Canticle "begins," says St. John, "with a person's initial steps in the service of God and continues until he reaches Spiritual Marriage, the ultimate state of perfection." The poem may therefore be broadly divided into three sections. (There is no strict time-sequence in the stanzas; nor is there a well-defined progression from one stage of the spiritual life to the next):

Stanzas 1–12: The first steps of the spiritual journey — the longings of impatient love.

Stanzas 13–21: The spiritual espousal, engagement; preparing for perfect union.

Stanzas 22–40: Perfect union; Spiritual Marriage. Longing for the Beatific Vision.

To a certain extent St. John repeats and elaborates the doctrine of *The Ascent of Mt. Carmel* and *The Dark Night,* but in a rather summary fashion; ordered descriptions of the various Nights of Sense and Spirit, even the terms, cannot be found. There is no specific treatment of the transitional stages, as we find in the earlier works. The Saint is not writing for beginners in the spiritual life, but, as he tells us in the Prologue, he writes for those who "have already experienced . . . mystical understanding." This "mystical wisdom comes through love" and is "given according to each one's capacity of spirit to accept in faith."

The intention is clear: to expound mystical doctrine to those who experience the call of God to divine intimacy. The commentary is autobiographical in the sense that the Saint is drawing on his own personal experience. He invites all to go to God by way of this mystical knowledge of Him, or contemplation; that all do not actually choose it is something that the Saint finds hard to explain. In *The Dark Night* (Book 1, chapter 9) he notes that God does not lead all souls by the road of contemplation, and only He knows why. Yet, he tells us, "a little of this pure love is more precious to God and the soul and more beneficial to the Church than all these works put together" (Stanza 29, paragraph 2). This "pure love" is that of the contemplative, who by God's gift has received the gift of a sweet and living knowledge, that "secret knowledge of god, mystical theology, contemplation" (Stanza 27, paragraph 5). In contemplation, "God teaches the soul very quietly and secretly, without its knowing how, without the sound of words, and without the help of any bodily or spiritual faculty, in silence and quietude, in darkness to all sensory and natural things". Some spiritual writers call this contemplation "knowing and un-knowing" (Stanza 39, paragraph 12).

It is this mysterious but real knowledge of God which St. John presents and explains to us in *The Spiritual Canticle*. It is not a way of spiritual consolations or extraordinary manifestations; it is certainly not a way of visions or revelations. These happen if God wills it, and St. John refers to, without describing, raptures and ecstasies which may occur at a certain stage. But like St. Teresa he is at pains to point out that these phenomena are not necessary, and should not be desired. If God allows them, they will be of profit to the person who receives them humbly. They are not in themselves signs of great holiness; rather they could be a proof of weakness. The Saint makes it clear that God draws each soul differently. He maps out a way to God of which he and many others have had personal experience, and he invites us to follow. It will be the way of the Cross, in which a certain darkness in faith is to be expected, and preferred "inasmuch as God does not communicate some supernatural light, He is intolerable darkness when He is near". We will know the sufferings of unrequited love, the seeming absence of God, the experience of His transcendence; but if we are courageous and persevering, there awaits us the ineffable joy of union with the Beloved. Beyond the Cross: resurrection, the lived experience of God's immanence of "God with us."

This intimacy with God, attainable in this life, is a foretaste of the

Beatific Vision: 'Although in Spiritual Marriage there is not the perfection of heavenly love, there is nonetheless a living and totally ineffable semblance of that perfection" (Stanza 38, paragraph 4). "It is not incredible . . . that she should understand, know and love in the Trinity, together with it, as does the Trinity itself! . . . It is for this that God created her in His image and likeness" (Stanza 39, paragraph 4). This gift of contemplation is not an end itself. Both St. John of the Cross and St. Teresa of Avila insist that it must always be directed to the good of the Church, and must be expresssed in a life of service to others: "This is the aim of prayer; this is the purpose of the Spiritual Marriage . . . good works and good works alone." Says St. Teresa, "You must not build upon the foundation of prayer and contemplation alone . . . strive after the virtues" (I.C.Mans. VII. 4). This is love-in-action; "contemplation combined with apostolic love" — in the words of the Vatican II Document for Religious *Perfectae Caritatis*.

In these days when so many people are searching for God in prayer, and when our youth are rejecting institutional religion and turning to Eastern mysticism for an authentic experience of the absolute, or the divine, it seems timely to make St. John of the Cross accessible to a greater number by presenting his teaching in a simplified form. In his works we find an approach to God which goes far to resolve the problem of the Deism, Existentialism and Atheism which has colored much of modern thinking about God. The God-Is-Dead school of the 1960s forced us to rethink, and it was right to emphasize that the kind of God which most people imagine does not, in fact, exist. St. John of the Cross insists on this too: we cannot imagine God, or form any conception of Him; He is wholly other, infinitely different— in a word, transcendent. But He is not inaccessible: God spoke to humankind in the Person of the Word Incarnate, "in whom was all the fullness of the Godhead" and who revealed to us the real nature of God's relationship with us—a relationship of love, of personal love for each one of us, His children. Not only is He our heavenly Father, but He, with the Son and the Holy Spirit, takes up His dwelling place in those who love Him. "If any man love me," said Jesus, "my Father will love him, and we shall come to him and make our dwelling place in him" (Jn. 14:23).

So God is not distant, or remote from us. We find Him within ourselves—as St. Teresa of Avila says, "in the little heaven of our own souls." It is the theme of *The Spiritual Canticle* that we can reach a degree of loving intimacy with God in this life that can be described fittingly only in the language of conjugal love. St. John of the Cross describes the spiritual journey in the burning words of a great lover of God, who speaks from experience and describes the astonishing intimacy of the Spiritual Marriage in language which draws its inspiration from the very love song of God to humankind, the Canticle of Canticles of the Old Testament.

All these place God in a new and exciting perspective for those who genuinely seek to experience Him in this way. None are excluded from setting out in quest of Him. "We are all," says St. Teresa of Avila, "by nature richly endowed, so as to have the power of holding converse with God himself." St. John of the Cross is eminently qualified to be our guide. Trained philosopher and theologian as he was, he has described, first in poetry (he has been acclaimed the greatest poet in the Spanish language), then in poetic prose, how all men of good will may come to know God in faith, and to love Him, and to communicate with Him in intimate, loving converse—not as yet "face to face", but in a communion of love which is a foreshadowing of the Beatific Vision, of eternal life, which is "knowing the Father, and Jesus Christ whom He has sent".

The prose commentary presented in this simplified version is a summary, or synopsis, of St. John's Second Redaction commentary. It retains the continuity of his thought, wording and expression, and I believe nothing of importance has been omitted. The aim has been to help the reader experiencing difficulty either in obtaining the original text or in reading it. It is hoped that the page-by-page explanation, the notes, will clarify the text.

This book is not intended to be a substitute for reading St. John of the Cross in the original text. The main purpose of the book is to encourage a fuller study of the works of St. John of the Cross and of St. Teresa of Avila, both Doctors of the Church, who speak to us so powerfully and with such authority of God and the things of God.

The reader should keep in mind that much of the poetic imagery of the poem was taken from the Song of Songs. Both poems take the form of a series of rapid dialogues between God and the souls (the bride). The poem, as presented here, is an original translation. The division of stanzas into three parts corresponds to that made by the Saint in "The Theme."

John Venard OCD

The Spiritual Canticle of St. John of the Cross is the only one of his works which covers the whole gamut of the spiritual life. It is hoped that this simplified version of his commentary on the poem, and the notes accompanying it, will provide an introduction to a reading of the actual text. This is a synopsis, not a series of quotations. The continuity of the Saint's thought is retained throughout.

Using St. John's own words, we may hope that what is here set down "not being fully explainable, may be read with a certain simplicity."

THE SPIRITUAL CANTICLE

Prologue

1.   It would be foolish to think
      that expressions of love
      arising from mystical understanding
      are fully explainable.
      However, "the Spirit of the Lord aids our weakness,
      pleading for us, that we may set forth
      what cannot be fully understood."
      That is why
      those who have experienced
      the secret mysteries of God
      try to express themselves
      by using figures and similes.
      If these are not read
      with a certain simplicity,
      they may seem absurdities,
      as in the comparisons
      drawn from the Song of Songs
      and other books of Holy Scripture.

2.   Therefore, there is no need
      to be bound by the explanations given here.
      Mystical wisdom, which comes through love,
      need not be understood distinctly;
      it is given according to each one's capacity of spirit
      to accept in faith.
      We love God, in faith,
      without understanding Him.

      I shall deal here
      only with the more extraordinary effects of prayer.
      There are many writings for beginners,
      and you for whom this is being written
      have already experienced
      the mystical understanding I have spoken of.

      I submit all my explanations
      to the judgement of the Church
      and I wish to explain the more difficult passages
      by reference to the Sacred Scriptures.

The Poem

I.
Stanzas 1–12
First steps of the spiritual journey—the longings of impatient love

1. Bride:
   Where have you hidden,
   Beloved, and left me with my grieving?
   You fled like a stag
   after wounding me;
   I went out calling you,
   and you were gone.

2. Shepherds, you that go
   up through the sheepfolds to the hill,
   if by chance you see
   him whom most I love,
   tell him that I am ailing, I suffer, and I die.

3. Seeking my love
   I will pass over the mountains
   and the river banks;
   I will not gather flowers,
   nor fear wild beasts;
   I will pass by strong men and frontiers.

4. O woods and thickets
   planted by the hand of my beloved!
   O meadow of green pasture,
   enameled bright with flowers,
   tell me, has he passed by you?

5. Scattering a thousand graces
   he passed by these groves in haste
   and looking on them as he went,
   with his glance alone
   he left them clothed in beauty.

6. Ah, who will be able to heal me?
   End by wholly surrendering yourself!
   Do not sent me any more messengers;
   they cannot tell me what I wish to hear.

7. All those who are free
   keep telling me a thousand graceful things of you.
   All wound me more,
   and a something I know not
   that they are stammering
   leaves me dying.

8. How do you endure,
   O life, not living where you live?
   the arrows you receive
   making you die
   from that which you conceive in you of your Beloved?

9. Why, since you wounded
   this heart, did you not heal it?
   And, since you stole it from me,
   why did you leave it so,
   not taking off what you have stolen?

10. Assuage these griefs of mine,
    since no one else can remove them;
    and may my eyes behold you,
    because you are their light,
    and I would open them to you alone.

11. Reveal your presence
    and may the vision of your beauty be my death.
    Behold! Love's sickness has no cure
    except your very presence and your image.

12. O Fount so crystal clear,
    if on your silvered face
    you suddenly would form
    those eyes so much desired
    which I hold deep designed within my heart!

II.
Stanzas 13–21
The spiritual espousal, engagement; preparing for perfect
union

13. Away with them, Beloved,
    for I am taking flight.
    (The spouse replies):
    Bridegroom:
    "Come back, my dove;
    the wounded stag
    appears upon the hill
    refreshed in the breeze of your flight."

14. My Beloved; the mountains,
    the lonely wooded valleys,
    the strange islands,
    the resounding streams,
    the whisper of love-laden airs.

15. The night serene,
    the time of rising dawn,
    the silent music,
    the sounding solitude,
    the supper which refreshes and increases love.

16. Drive off those little foxes,
    for our vineyard is now in flower,
    while we make a pine-like cluster of roses;
    and let no one appear on the hill.

17. Be still, deadening north wind;
    come, south wind. You that waken love,
    breathe through my garden;
    let its scented fragrance flow,
    and the beloved will feed amid the flowers.

18. You nymphs of Judea,
    while among flowers and roses
    the amber spreads its perfume,
    stay away, there on the outskirts:
    desire not to touch our thresholds.

19.   Hide yourself, my love;
    turn your face to gaze upon the mountains,
    think not to speak;
    but look at those companions
    going with her through strange islands.

20.   Bridegroom:
    Swift-winged birds,
    lions, stags, and leaping roes,
    mountains, lowlands, and river banks,
    waters, winds, and heat of the day
    watching terrors of the night:

21.   By the pleasant lyres
    and the siren's song, I conjure you,
    cease your anger
    and touch not the wall,
    that the bride may sleep secure.

III.
Stanzas 22–40
Perfect union; Spiritual Marriage. Longing for the Beatific
Vision.

22.   The bride has entered
    the sweet garden so much desired,
    and she rests to her delight,
    reclining her neck
    on the gentle arms of her beloved.

23.   Beneath the apple tree
    there you were betrothed to me;
    there I gave you my hand
    and you were raised up again,
    where your mother lost her maidenhood.

24.   Bride:
    Our flowery bed,
    bound with dens of lions,
    is hung with purple,
    built up in peace,
    and crowned with a thousand shields of gold.

25. Following your footsteps
    maidens run along the way;
    at the touch of a spark,
    the spiced wine,
    flowings from the balsam of God.

26. In the inner wine cellar
    I drank of my beloved, and when I went abroad,
    through all this valley
    I no longer knew anything
    and lost the flock which I was following.

27. There he gave me his breast;
    there he taught me a knowledge, very sweet,
    and I gave myself to him,
    withholding nothing;
    there I promised to be his bride.

28. Now I occupy my soul
    and all that I possess in serving him;
    I no longer tend the flock,
    nor have I any other work
    now that I practice love, and that alone.

29. If, then, I am no longer
    seen or found on the common,
    you will say that I am lost;
    that, wandering love-stricken
    I lost my way, and was found.

30. With flowers and emeralds
    gathered on cold mornings
    we shall weave garlands
    flowering in your love
    and bound with one hair of mine.

31. That single hair of mine
    waving on my neck has caught your eye;
    you gazed at it upon my neck,
    and by it captive you were held
    and one of my eyes has wounded you.

32.   When you looked at me
      your eyes imprinted your grace in me;
      for this you loved me ardently,
      and this my eyes deserved—
      to adore what they beheld in you.

33.   Despise me not;
      for if before you found me dark,
      now truly you can look at me,
      since having looked at me
      in me you left your grace and beauty.

34.   Bridegroom:
      The small white dove
      has returned to the ark with an olive branch,
      and now the turtle dove
      has found its longed-for mate
      by the green river banks.

35.   She lived in solitude
      and now in solitude has built her nest;
      and in solitude her dear one alone guides her,
      who also bears in solitude
      the wound of love.

36.   Bride:
      Let us rejoice, Beloved,
      and let us go forth to behold ourselves in your beauty
      to the mountain and to the hill,
      to where the pure water flows,
      and further let us enter deep into the thicket.

37.   And then we will go on
      to the high caverns in the rock
      which are so well concealed;
      there we shall enter
      and taste the fresh juice of the pomegranates.

38.   There you will show me
      what my soul has been seeking.
      And then you will give me,
      you, my life, will give me there
      what you gave me on that other day.

39.   The breathing of the air,
       the song of the sweet nightingale,
       the grove and its living beauty,
       in the serene night,
       with a flame that consumes and gives no pain.

40.   No one looked at it
       nor did Aminadab appear;
       the siege was still;
       and the cavalry,
       at the sight of the waters, descended.

THE THREE DIVISIONS, WITH STANZA HEADINGS

I.
Stanzas 1–12
First steps of the spiritual journey—the
longings of impatient love

Stanza 1:   Anxious searching, longing for God.
       2:   Intercessory prayer; the aid of "intermediaries" is sought.
       3:   Mortification of the natural affections.
       4:   Knowledge of God in His Creation.
       5:   The grandeur of God as revealed in Creation.
       6:   Longing for God's presence; signs do not satisfy.
       7:   Longing for a knowledge of God in His mysteries.
       8:   Conflict, tension; life as it is in contrast to real life in God, so much desired.
       9:   Longing to be possessed by God.
     10:   Everything but God is torment.
     11:   If only God would reveal himself!
     12:   Seeking the Beloved in faith.

II.
Stanzas 13–21
The spiritual espousal, engagement; preparing
for perfect union

Stanza 13:   Suffering—the Passive Night of the Spirit— God's seeming absence.
  14–15:   Joy follows suffering: beginning of the spiritual espousal; communion and exchange of love.
     16:   Peace in the nearness of the Beloved; consciousness of virtues, along with sensual temptation.
     17:   Spiritual dryness gives way to the peace of the Holy Spirit, communicating the Bridegroom.
     18:   May the higher, spiritual nature dominate the unruly sensual appetites and desires.
     19:   May the spiritual communications of the Beloved be communicated to the spirit alone, not to the senses.
  20–21:   The natural appetites and passions are brought under control; peace results.

III.

Stanzas 22–40

Perfect union, Spiritual Marriage. Longing for
the Beatific Vision.

Stanza 22: Liberation; beginning of total transformation in
the Beloved; loving intimacy.

23: The mystery of the Incarnation is revealed.

24: The Bridegroom communicates His own love
and His own virtues, with peace and
tranquillity.

25: The benefits devout souls receive from the
Beloved—Divine touches, inebriation of the
Holy Spirit.

26: Transformation in God in the substance of the
soul; the action of the Holy Spirit, bringing
about complete detachment.

27: God's communication of himself in tenderness
and love; mutual surrender.

28: Love equalizes; love alone achieves surrender;
habitual and loving attentiveness to God's will.

29: Pure love, not activities, is important to God;
total withdrawal in nakedness of spirit.

30: Mutual exchange of virtues—God and the soul.

31: God is captivated by the soul's faith and
virtues, which are the work of the Holy Spirit,
yet merited.

32: All is God's doing; nothing is attibuted to the
soul.

33: Contrasts the soul's former state with what God
has perfected in her; always the Divine
initiative.

34: The Bridegroom praises the bride's desire for
solitude.

35: Peaceful solitude; liberty of spirit under the
guidance of the Bridegroom.

36: The soul's only activity—surrender. The beauty
of God is savored and shared. She asks to
share the secrets of the Beloved.

37: Sharing the Bridegroom's knowledge of the
mysteries of the Incarnation.

38: The soul asks for a love as perfect as the
Bridegroom's.

39: Looking forward to the Beatific Vision; breathing of the Holy Spirit, participation in God.

40: Perfect detachment achieved, the devil conquered; expectation of the Beatific Vision.

ABOUT THIS BOOK

The left-hand pages contain, in simplified form, the continuous summary of *The Spiritual Canticle* as written by St. John of the Cross. This text is a commentary on a stanza or stanzas (as in 14, 15, and 20, 21) of the poem. Usually the Saint prepared the reader for the commentary by writing an introduction, or "annotation," and inserting it immediately before the stanza. In some cases, he omitted this introduction.

The right-hand page consists of Father John Venard's notes, which explain the original text found on the facing, left-hand page. The reader is urged to refer to the complete text of *The Spiritual Canticle* after studying each passage, in order to savor the fullness of the Saint's thought.

Abbreviations

Asc.	=	*The Ascent of Mount Carmel*
D.N.	=	*The Dark Night*
L.F.	=	*The Living Flame of Love*
S.C.	=	*The Spiritual Canticle*
W.P.	=	*The Way of Perfection* (St. Teresa)
I.C.	=	*The Interior Castle* (St. Teresa)
Mans.	=	*Mansions* (in references to I.C.)

THE THEME

(in the words of St. John of the Cross)

1. These stanzas begin with a person's initial steps in the service of God and continue until he reaches Spiritual Marriage, the ultimate state of perfection. They refer, consequently, to the three stages or ways of spiritual exercise (purgative, illuminative, and unitive) through which a person passes in his advance to this state, and they describe some of the characteristics and effects of these ways.

2. The initial stanzas treat of the state of beginners, that of the purgative way. (Stanzas 1–12)

    The subsequent ones deal with the state of proficients in which the spiritual espousal is effected, that is, of the illuminative way. (Stanzas 13–21)

    The stanzas following these refer to the unitive way, that of the perfect, where the Spiritual Marriage takes place. This unitive way of the perfect follows the illuminative way of the proficients. (Stanzas 22–35)

    The final stanzas of the beatific state, the sole aspiration of a person who has reached perfection. (Stanzas 36–40)

    The beginning of the commentary on the love songs between the bride and Christ, the Bridegroom.

DIVISION I

FIRST STEPS OF THE SPIRITUAL JOURNEY

Introduction

The soul realizes
the shortness of life (Job 14:5),
that the path leading to eternal life
is narrow (Mt. 7:14),
that the just man
is saved with difficulty (1 Pet. 4:18),
that the things of this world
are vain and deceitful (Eccl. 1:2),
that all things come to an end
like falling water (2Kgs. 14:14).
She recalls God's goodness,
His creation, His gift of life, Redemption,
and her obligation to respond in love.
She remembers her own ingratitude,
her own worldliness,
causing God to be far away.
So, remembering
that the day is far spent (Lk. 24:29),
and that she must render
an account of everything,
even to the last farthing (Mt. 5:26),
and wounded now with love for God,
she calls out to Him, her Beloved:

"Where have you hidden,
Beloved, and left me with my grieving?
You fled like a stag
after wounding me;
I went out calling you,
and you were gone."

Theme: Anxious searching, longing for God.

1.   These few introductory words seem to indicate that the period of preparation during which one meditates on the truths revealed in Scripture, the shortness of life, and God's goodness is quite short; after, the soul "is wounded with love." In fact, this period may be short or long depending on the will of God and our good will and generosity.

St. John presupposes familiarity with the teaching of *The Ascent of Mount Carmel* and *The Dark Night*, and the need for purification and trials in the early stages of the spiritual life. He states in the opening sentence of *The Ascent* that we can reach divine union "quickly", if we learn to "live in complete nakedness and freedom of spirit." Nevertheless it is normally a gradual development. Cf. Asc. II.17. The subjects of meditation here proposed are not for the early stages only; no matter how advanced we may be in the spiritual life we must from time to time reflect on these mysteries (Asc. II: 15.1, 17.7).

Characteristic of the attitude of mind in these early stages is a certain fear of God, of His judgements, of final retribution; thoroughly scriptural, it offsets a false notion of freedom leading to permissiveness. "These reflections," St. Teresa says, "vanquish the devils" (Mans. II.1).

Commentary

2.   The soul,
     enamored of the Word, her Bridegroom,
     expresses her longings,
     complaining of His absence.

3.   *"Where have you hidden?":*
     She seeks clear and essential vision
     and possession of the Divine Essence:
     the Word of God
     "in the bosom of the Father" [Jn. 1:18].
     This is hidden from human understanding.
     "Truly You are a hidden God" [Is. 45:15].
     No sublime communication or sensible awareness
     of God's nearness
     is a sure testimony of His presence.
     However sublime our knowledge of God,
     these experiences are not God.
     He still remains hidden in the soul.

4.   Neither is dryness nor lack of experience
     a reflection of His absence.
     There can be no certain knowledge
     from such experiences
     that one is in God's grace;
     neither can we be certain
     that we lack God's grace
     if we have no such "experience" of His presence.
     So the soul does not ask for sensible devotion.

5.   Cf. Cant. 1:6:
     "Show me where you (the Father) pasture (in the Son),
     where you rest (in the Son),
     at midday (for eternity)."
     She is seeking her Bridegroom
     where the Father feeds in infinite glory.

2–4.   We seek God himself in the Person of the Risen Christ, not
         merely signs of God in the outer senses. In one sentence St.
         John gives us the true notion of faith: the possession in Love
         of the person of the Word of God, who brings us with Him
         (and this is the work of the Holy Spirit), into the bosom of
         the Father (Asc. II: 23.3). Cf. Stanza 12.4: "Faith gives us God
         . . . it gives Him to us *truly*. " Here "vision" means "seeing"
         in the biblical sense—taking hold of, possessing: "He who sees
         me, sees the Father." This is emphatically not a vision in the
         sense of "apparition." Here is stated categorically the teaching
         set out so forcefully in *The Ascent*: nothing but faith can give
         us, in this life, God himself. In this sense He always remains
         hidden (Asc. II.9), no matter how exalted our union with Him.
         Despite our feelings, or awareness of His presence, or sublime
         communications, we cannot be sure of His presence. We should
         not be discouraged if these things never occur; we must not
         conclude from this that He is absent.

         So the ground is cleared at the beginning: there must be no
         desire at all for sensible devotion; no lurking desire for some
         revelation, a vision perhaps, or some feeling of consolation
         from time to time, to "strengthen our faith." If God gives
         consolations, or revelations, that is His doing; it is the desire
         for these which St. John condemns. Read Asc. II.16–21.

5.   From all eternity and for all eternity the Father gives birth to
         the Son, to whom He never ceases to communicate himself
         and in whom He finds His rest. It is here, in the Trinity, that
         we are to seek the Word, the Bridegroom. The whole spiritual
         journey is the deepening of a love relationship in faith, with
         the Word, Christ, the Son of God, in His Sacred Humanity, and
         through Him to the Father, by the action of the Holy Spirit
         (cf. "By Him, with Him, in Him . . ." of the Canon of the Mass).
         The word "Bridegroom": Do we at this stage think so intimately
         of Christ? The answer is that the term is used in anticipation
         of the reality to come, of that deep, loving intimacy for which
         even now we experience the longing, as from afar.

21

6.   *"Where have you hidden?":*
Where is the Spouse most surely hidden?
The Word, the Son of God,
together with the Father and the Holy Spirit,
is hidden by His essence and His presence
in the innermost being of the soul.
A person should leave all things
through affection and will,
enter within himself
in deepest recollection,
and regard things as though non-existent.
Cf. St. Augustine:
"I wrongly sought You without, Lord
who were within."

7.   So, you yourself are His dwelling place;
"Behold, the kingdom of God is within you" [Lk. 17:21].
"You are the temple of God" [2 Cor. 6:16].

8.   Therefore, be glad;
desire Him there, adore Him there.
You will only become distracted and wearied
by seeking Him outside of yourself.
The difficulty is that He is hidden . . .
but you must know where He hides,
and search with assuredness.

6.   From afar? Yet He is so near. With St. Augustine, quoted so
        often by St. Teresa in this context, we make the astonishing,
        delightful discovery: God is not far away, in the heavens, infinitely
        distant; He is within us! This discovery gives the reality of God-
        in-us, and gives meaning to the "detachment" insisted on
        constantly by St. John of the Cross.

        To find Him within, we must leave all things, in the sense
        of removing obstacles to God's loving action, putting aside any
        voluntary, wilful, inordinate, unmortified desire or attachment
        for any person, place, or thing which we know is keeping us
        from God. If our efforts are constant and sincere, we will be
        able to enter within ourselves, finding God there, in the depths
        of the soul. This detachment is not a burdensome thing; it
        consists in the quiet determination to put away whatever keeps
        us from God. Not every pleasure of the sense does this; with
        discernment we must know ourselves, remembering that what
        might for another be harmful or an attachment may not be
        so for us (and vice versa). It is certainly not meant to take
        the joy out of life. On the contrary, we know the joy of true
        freedom of the children of God (cf. Asc. I.2).

7–8.   Here is cause for rejoicing; the Word of God assures us of
        His presence within us: we are "temples of God" (1 Cor. 6:19).
        We know with certainty that He is there, in the "little heaven
        of our souls", as St. Teresa says. Here is the foundation of
        all Teresian prayer, entering by faith into the Interior Castle,
        "nothing other than ourselves," finding God there, loving Him
        there, "desiring Him there, adoring Him there."

9.   You inquire:
        "Why then don't I find Him,
        experience Him?"

        Answer:
        "He remains concealed;
        but you do not conceal yourself
        in order to encounter and experience Him."

        Just as the wise man [Matt. 13:44]
        sold all his possessions
        so you must forget possessions,
        and hide in the interior chamber of your spirit.
        There, "pray to your Father in secret,
        closing the door behind you"
        —in hiding, that is, in a way
        transcending all language and feeling.

9.   Here the practical man poses the question "If He is there, why don't I have some experience of His presence?" The answer: We have already said that He is hidden, and we must not expect to know except by faith that He is present. We must hide ourselves, as He does—hide ourselves in faith, happy to be in a certain darkness regarding God's presence and hide ourselves also in the sense that we really try to detach ourselves from the things in our life that keep us from God, such as a habit of sin, deliberate imperfections, selfishness, intolerance, jealousies, indulgence in unnecessary comfort or luxury. We must find out the thing in our lives which is a self-indulgence, and mortify it. In these ways, we will "be hidden".

Possessions, i.e. unmortified attachments. But how can we "forget" them? How can we "forget creatures"? Isn't this selfish? Doesn't it conflict with the need to love everyone, to see good in the world, and in all material things? There is no conflict. We are talking only about possessions, things, creatures, people, who prevent us in some way from coming to God. Second objection: What of the community and liturgical dimension of prayer; isn't there over-emphasis on "praying in secret"? Answer: There are two kinds of prayer: personal, as mentioned here, "in secret"; and "praying together," especially the common prayer of liturgical celebration. St. John of the Cross is treating only of personal union, knowing full well that the person who achieves this by the grace of God is the very person who will understand and appreciate the full meaning and significance of liturgical prayer in common. The truth is that liturgy has meaning only for those who are first disposed for it by personal prayer apart from the liturgy. Prayer in common, in turn, stimulates private prayer; both are necessary and complement and enrich each other.

10   Cf. Isaias 26:20:
"Come, enter your secret chambers,
shut the door behind you,
hide yourself a little, even for a moment";
that is, during this life—a moment.
If we do this, "I shall give you hidden treasures
and reveal to you
the substance and mysteries of secrets" [Isaias 45:3],
that is, of God himself;
who is the substance and concept of faith.
Faith is the secret and the mystery
to be uncovered in the perfect vision of God
[1 Cor. 13:10].

Never in this mortal life
will the uncovering of these mysteries be perfect;
but the soul will merit the high perfection
of the union with the Son of God—
transformation, through love,
in Him, her Spouse.

10.   We pray in this way, that is, in a way "transcending all language and feeling", without effort at forming considerations, "making meditation," or using the imagination and the intellect laboriously; we enter upon an act of general, peaceful, loving, tranquil knowledge (cf. Asc. II.14) in faith, which gives God Himself. In the next life, faith will give way to vision. St. John of the Cross insists that never in this life can the vision of God be perfect, but the eventual transformation of the soul into God is a reality. It is something that is merited in the sense that once the obstacles to union with God are removed, transformation into God will surely take place. Again the Saint anticipates. This transformation is the culmination of the journey; but "God is faithful." He always does His part.

Does this mean, then, that if we remain in a state of mediocrity in the spiritual life, there is something lacking in us? Both St. John of the Cross and St. Teresa would answer "Yes": it means that we refuse to take up the cross of detachment and the effort needed to practice the ordinary, everyday virtues of the Christian life; a refusal to accept the Cross of the sufferings of body or spirit which God allows and which are necessary purification; a refusal to accept the darkness of faith, hoping for consolations in prayer, revelations of some kind, and so on. Both St. Teresa and St. John of the Cross deal at some length with this problem of why so few attain the transformation we speak of, though many do enter the higher ways, only to turn back through lack of courage, generosity, and determination: "There are very few who do not enter these [Fifth] Mansions" (I.C. Mans. V.1).

11.   So, seek Him in faith and love
        which are like the guides of a blind man,
        leading along an unknown path,
        to the place where God is hidden.

        Faith is like the feet
        by which one journeys to God,
        and love is like one's guide.
        The soul will merit through love
        the discovery of the content of faith,
        that is, the Bridegroom;
        here, through divine union,
        hereafter, through essential vision
        in glory, "face to face" (1 Cor. 13:12).
        But, no matter how close
        the union in this life,
        He always remains hidden
        in the bosom of the Father.

11.   Continued emphasis on faith and love; we move ahead in
        darkness, being content to love without seeking consolation
        of "seeing," or feeling God's presence. The Bridegroom always
        remains hidden. Let it be remembered, though, that the darkness,
        or, better, the obscurity of faith, is a real experience of God,
        not just a void; God is known to be present, but is seemingly
        absent. This is a real awareness, not just a vague feeling.
        Reaffirmed with insistence is St. John of the Cross's teaching
        that the object or content of faith, that which it contains (and
        gives) is the Bridegroom himself; not only doctrines, or truths,
        but the Person, truth itself. In this the Saint anticipates the
        rediscovery in our time of the real meaning of faith—a dynamic,
        living relationship in Love with a Person. Cf. Vat. II: "By Faith
        . . . man entrusts his whole self freely to God" (*Dei Verbum*
        5). Cf Stanza 12.4–6.

        Faith, for St. John of the Cross, is an experience of God; it
        is a mystical experience, or "mystical intelligence, which is
        confused and obscure" (Asc. II.24.4). It is "infused contemp-
        lation" (D.N. I.10.6). "through which God Himself is
        experienced" (S.C. 12.4). Belief, then, in the truths of faith,
        is absolutely necessary, but it is the necessary means to the
        end, the object of our faith, "the content of our faith, the
        Bridegroom" (*text*). It is a life, lived out in love; it is living
        divinely, in Christ (cf. Gal. 5:6: "faith, working through love").
        "Come to me," Jesus said; "I am the Way, the Truth, and the
        Life; and "I have come that they may have life." It is impossible
        to read St. John of the Cross, and really understand him, if
        we limit his notion of faith, which is totally Christ-centered.
        We arrive at a faith which is simple contemplation in Love
        of a Person—without images, concepts, forms, ideas. Cf. St.
        John's Gospel 20:30: "that believing, you may have life in His
        name."

12.   So seek Him always as one hidden
        and thus you exalt God
        and approach near to Him.
        Pay no attention
        to what your faculties can grasp,
        not desiring satisfaction
        in what you understand about God,
        but in what you do not understand about Him;
        seek Him in faith,
        He who is hidden,
        and seek Him in a secret way.
        Do not think that
        because you do not understand,
        taste, or experience Him,
        He is far away, or concealed.
        The less distinct your understanding of Him,
        the closer you approach Him.
        "He made darkness
        His hiding place" (Ps. 17:12).
        Consider Him as hidden at all times.

13.   *"Where have you hidden,*
        Beloved, and left me with my grieving?":
        When God is really loved,
        He readily answers
        the request of the one who loves Him.
        "If you abide in me,
        ask whatever you desire . . ." (Jn. 15:7).
        We can call God 'Beloved'
        if we are wholly with Him,
        if we do not allow our hearts
        to be attached to anything outside of Him,
        and if we ordinarily
        center our thoughts on Him.
        Keep your spirit continually with God,
        your heart lovingly
        and entirely set on Him.
        Nothing is obtained from God
        except by love.

12.   Perhaps it is the Saint's experience in directing others that makes
       him so emphatic, to the point of being repetitious, with regard
       to faith. The demand is total: ". . . seek Him always . . . Pay
       no attention to what your faculties can grasp." Surely this is
       another reason why so many of us falter on the way; we never
       really accept this in practice in our own lives. We insist on
       seeking some spiritual satisfaction or consolation, or at least
       we hope for something of this kind. We want to "understand
       about God," but the time having come to leave formal
       meditations, God wants us to open up our hearts quite simply
       to the action of the Holy Spirit, who "helps us in our weakness
       when we do not know how to pray" (Rom. 8:26).

       At this stage, we should "pay no attention to discursive
       meditation, allowing the soul to remain in rest and quietude,
       even though we seem to be doing nothing and wasting time;
       and even though we think this disinclination to think about
       anything is due to laxity . . . we must be content simply with
       a loving and peaceful attentiveness to God, and live without
       the effort and the desire to taste or feel Him" (D.N. II.10.4).
       See Asc. XIII.14 for the "signs by which we will know that we
       are to pray as above, to enter the 'Night of the Soul.'"

13.   In chapter VII of *The Way of Perfection*, St. Teresa says that
       endearing words should be kept for the Spouse, Christ, alone.
       St. John of the Cross reminds us that we cannot use the term
       "Beloved" of God unless, totally given to Him, we have no
       unmortified attachments, and our thoughts are ordinarily
       centered on Him. This should be properly understood. We
       cannot, in the midst of busy occupations, always be actually
       thinking of God. But God is never far from our thoughts, and
       from time to time we consciously think of Him or speak to
       Him. In the beginning this habit of the presence of God is
       acquired by frequent effort; as time goes on the conscious effort
       to recall God becomes unnecessary—God becomes as it were,
       the atmosphere in which we live and move. Our hearts are
       "lovingly and entirely set on Him" (*text*). God is always the
       point of reference in everything we do, every decision we make.
       Then, "if you abide in me [in this way], ask whatever you desire
       and it shall be given to you." St. Teresa explains "the nature
       of this holy companionship in *The Way of Perfection*—how
       we "retire within ourselves even during our ordinary
       occupations" (W.P. XXIX).

14.   *"and left me with my grieving":*
    This is how we recognize
    the person who loves God—
    she is content with nothing less than God.
    Satisfaction of heart
    is not possessing things
    but in being stripped of them,
    in poverty of spirit.
    Perfection of love consists
    in this poverty of spirit
    in which God is possessed
    (not, however, completely in this life).
    Cf. David Ps. 16:15:
    "When your glory appears I shall be filled."
    "Grieving" is connected with hope
    (Cf. Rom. 8:23: "We ourselves
    who have the first fruits of the Spirit
    groan within ourselves,
    hoping for the adoption of the sons of God").
    The soul, have tasted of the sweetness
    of God's communication at some time,
    cries out, suffering His absence.

15.   *"You fled like a stag":*
    The stag, withdrawn, solitary,
    comes and disappears swiftly (Cant. 2:9).
    God usually visits devout souls
    in order to regale and uplift them,
    then leaves, in order
    to try, humble, and teach them.

16.   *"after wounding me":*
    That is, with a deeper wound of love
    than that of your absence;
    increasing my desire
    You flee, resting not even for a moment.

14.   "To come to possess all, desire the possession of nothing" (Asc. I.3.11). All, Nothing: God is the All and the Saint helps us to recognize whether we truly love Him. If we were to ask ourselves "What do I want most?', the answer would not be "God, but in the next life", but "God, here and now." All Carmelite spirituality is contained in that; in the desire for Divine intimacy, now; the possession of God, "nothing less than God," which will make us courageous enough, if our motive is right, to strip ourselves and be stripped by God of anything that is an obstacle to love of Him.

What is the right motive? St. John (Asc. I.13.4) tells us: "Do all this for the love of Jesus Christ." He might well have said, instead of "satisfaction of heart," "true freedom of heart." St. Francis of Assisi knew what it was to be truly free when he dispossessed himself of everything, and St. John of the Cross speaks also of the dispossession of spiritual goods, revelations, and so on, even when they come from God (cf. Asc. II.11).

In this poverty of spirit we have the right to hope (with that certainty which is the note of Christian hope) for the possession of God. Darkness, dryness of spirit, the seeming absence of the Beloved, are a true experience of God: "God values in you an inclination to aridity and suffering for love of Him more than all possible consolations, spiritual visions, and meditations" (*Saying of St. John of the Cross* 14). In *The Ascent* he lists the reasons for not desiring extraordinary "experiences": this desire weakens our faith, hinders detachment, prevents us from arriving at the truly spiritual; we become less receptive of true devotion and are easily deceived by the devil (Asc. II.11).

15–16. All this is not darkness; it usually happens (note "usually") that God gives us some brief, fleeting evidence of His presence— but only for a moment, then He is gone. The mere "touch" of the Divine inflames and uplifts us; but the light becomes darkness again, and we are humbled in spirit, and learn in the school of self-knowledge how little we can do without Him. The desire for the Beloved increases.

17.   Besides these visits,
        God usually grants
        secret touches of His love,
        piercing, wounding, cauterizing;
        so inflaming
        that the will burns up in this flame,
        a consuming fire, renewing wholly,
        changing the manner of its being,
        like the phoenix
        rising, reborn, from its ashes (Ps. 72.21):
        "My heart was inflamed; I have been changed,
        brought to nothing, and I knew it not."

18, 19. *"after wounding me"*:
        These visits do not refresh and satisfy;
        rather, they heal and afflict
        more than they satisfy,
        stimulating the sorrow and longing to see God.

17.   The poetic language here should not mislead us into thinking
        that there must then be some kind of spectacular evidence
        of God's presence or action in the soul. Sometimes it may
        happen in this way; God treats each soul differently. The key
        words of this passage are "secret", "renewal" and "reborn;"
        the work of the Holy Spirit in us is constant renewal, a re-
        creation with every new infusion of grace.

        If this is true of all the baptized, who are "born again" (Jn. 3),
        it is not surprising that if (as presumed here) we have resolved
        to give ourselves totally to god, our whole way of life will be
        changed and a completely new realization of who we are before
        God will follow from the Holy Spirit's intensive action in us,
        leading us on lovingly to intimacy with God. This may happen
        either suddenly or gradually: "The Spirit breathes where He
        will."

18–19. Lest one should think that these touches of God are sweet
        and refreshing, we are reminded that the effect is just the
        opposite. All may happen in great dryness of spirit, without
        apparent consolation; but these "visits" of God stimulate us
        in our good desires.

20.   *"I went out calling you,*
and you were gone":
This spiritual departure
refers to the two ways
of going after God:
a departure from all things,
in contempt of them;
self-forgetfulness,
achieved by the love of God,
when the love of God
really touches the soul.

21.   *"and you were gone"*:
I desired you, but did not find you;
there are now no supports,
natural or divine,
or so it seems (Cant. 3:2, 5:7).
The absence of the Beloved
causes constant sufferings.

20.   We have to give up, or depart from, all things and forget self.
        We moderns do not like the term "contempt of all things" (the
        Saint actually says *por desprecio y aborrecimiento de todas
        las cosas*, which is even stronger). The modern attitude, very
        commendable, of seeing good in everything in God's Creation
        seems to conflict with "abhorring all things." In this context,
        always reading "all things which, by their wrongful use, would
        keep us from loving God" will give us the Saint's thought
        correctly throughout his writings. Chapter 12, Book I, of *The
        Ascent* should be read in this context. Perhaps no one revelled
        in the good things of God's Creation more than St. John of
        the Cross (as we shall see later).

        Self-forgetfulness is achieved, not in a negative fashion, but
        positively. It is not that we forget self, then try to love God;
        it is the reverse. We first love God, and forgetfulness of self
        follows. The Saint goes on to suggest that this is the work
        of God; the love of God "touches the soul" and we are impelled
        to stop thinking of ourselves. The positive effort of withdrawing
        from natural inclinations and supports will no longer be
        necessary: God "draws us away" (cf. "Draw us, we will run
        after you" (Song of Songs)). Cf. St. Teresa's formula for acquiring
        humility: "Fix your eyes on God; thus you will realize its [your
        soul's] own baseness better than by thinking of its own nature."
        (Mans. I.2).

21.   The emphasis is on suffering. All seems lost. At this point many
        lay down the Cross, and go no further. St. Teresa has sound
        advice for those in this state: "The soul will certainly suffer
        great trials at this time . . . the Cross which your Spouse bore
        upon His shoulders is yours to carry too; all that the beginner
        in prayer has to do . . . is to labor and be resolute and prepare
        himself . . . to bring his will into conformity with the will of
        God. This is the very greatest perfection" (I.C. Mans. II.1). It
        is not simply dryness, aridity in prayer, which is the suffering;
        the sure sign that we are on the right path is that what causes
        the distress is the apparent absence of the Beloved. This is
        really an experience of God's transcendence: He seems to be
        absent, remote, infinitely distant; the felt experience of His
        immanence is yet to come.

        Cf. Asc. II.7: "The one thing necessary is seriously to deny oneself
        both interiorly and exteriorly, to be ready to suffer for the sake
        of Christ and to die to oneself in all things."

22.   She is surrendered to the Beloved,
but He does not surrender to her.
She suffers immeasurably;
the will is healthy,
the spirit cleansed,
and well prepared for God;
an immense good is shown her,
but not granted to her.
The pain is unspeakable.

22. To have come thus far is no small achievement, no small grace. We fail to recognize this, not realizing how much God has done. Many people, excellently disposed, who truly want to love God, "their will healthy and the spirit cleansed," need to be assured at this stage that all is well. So far from going backwards, all is progress, and they should have confidence, waiting simply on God, "in silence and hope" despite the pain and darkness.

"Shepherds, you that go
up through the sheepfolds to the hill,
if by chance you see
him whom most I love
tell him that I am ailing, I suffer, and I die."

Commentary

1.   The soul desires
intercessors, intermediaries—
her desires, affections, moanings—
to manifest her love.

2.   These are *"shepherds"*,
pasturing, feeding the soul
with spiritual goods,
and by means of these yearnings
God communicates himself—
not otherwise.

3.   *"Sheepfolds"*: the choirs of angels,
intermediaries, to the "hill," God
(cf. Tob. 12:12).

Theme: Intercessory prayer; the aid of "intermediaries" is sought.

1.   We feel helpless, disconsolate; we are the lover who thinks that his is an unrequited love. But the lover is ever resourceful; he asks others to carry his message of love. We feel this love, and must express it; with desires and affections of the heart, we tell God of our love, and it is pleasing to Him. He responds, with a certain "giving" of himself, to these imperfect, but loving advances.

2.   Thus love grows through the exercise of the virtue. Hence the value, at this and at every stage, of the simple prayer or aspiration of love often repeated: "My God, I love you."

3.   St. John assures us that the angels are our messengers, bringing our love to God, and encouraging and inspiring us to continue in the quest for God. This, by definition, is what an angel is— a messenger; one who communicates between God and men, and men and God.

4, 5.   *"If by chance you see*
         him whom most I love":
         If the time is at hand,
         God always answers our prayer,
         but only when
         the time, season, circumstance, has arrived.
         Compare Exodus, wherein the Israelites prayed
         for four hundred years.

6.   *"tell him that I am ailing,*
         I suffer, and I die":
         I suffer in intellect, will, and memory—
         in the intellect,
         lacking the vision of God;
         in the will,
         lacking the possession of God;
         in the memory,
         remembering the lack
         of both these blessings.

4–6.   We make our request with all the insistence of lovers who
         can brook no denial; this is very pleasing to God. "Ask and
         you shall receive, seek and you shall find," of the Gospel, implies
         that we must be persistent in prayer to the point of importunity.
         Asking in this way is proof of our good dispositions; how much
         more when we ask for the very gift God wishes to give us,
         His love? Cf. Luke 11:13: "How much more will your Heavenly
         Father give the Holy Spirit to those who ask Him." The Holy
         Spirit, Love, in Person! God never refuses a request for a spiritual
         gift, for a grace; we can be certain of this. He may refuse our
         request for a material thing, at a particular time, but the request
         for love of Him, more love, never goes unanswered.

         Nevertheless, St. John impresses on us that God answers in
         His own time, in His own way—"if the time is at hand." Like
         Jesus in the Garden, we always have this proviso in mind:
         "Father, if it is your will . . ." (Lk. 21:42).

         There is a sense of urgency in our request—that the angels
         carry the message to God that with all the powers of our soul
         we long for Him and suffer because of His absence.

43

7.   The soul merely discloses her need—
        compare the Blessed Virgin at Cana,
        and Martha and Mary,
        "He whom you love is sick."
        The reasons for this are:
        the Lord knows what is suitable for us
        better than we do;
        the Lord has more compassion
        when He finds resignation
        in the soul;
        the soul is safeguarded
        against self-love and possessiveness.
        Hence, she says,
        "Tell him that
        I am ailing (He is my health),
        I suffer (He is my joy), *and*
        I die (He is my life)."

7.   Still more practical advice on prayer, and answers to prayer. The prayer of the Blessed Virgin at Cana indicates how pleasing to God is the simplicity of heart and the immense confidence shown when we simply place our need before God. "They have no wine"; it was not Mary's stated request but her whole attitude of mind and heart, of perfect trust that Jesus would do whatever was needed, that caused Him to work the miracle, even though He did not seem to want to! Similarly Martha and Mary: "He [Lazarus] whom you love, is sick." St. John gives three reasons for the power of such prayer, very practical and "down to earth."

"Tell him that I am ailing, I suffer, and I die"; there is great distress, but no loss of hope. He is there; He is always faithful. Cf. St. Paul; "I know in whom I have believed" (2 Tim 1:12).

This brings us to an important truth about prayer: it consists not in what we say, the words we use, or what we are thinking about; the success of our prayer does not depend on whether we are able to concentrate or on whether we succeed in controlling our imagination, but in our disposition, our attitude of mind and heart. The prayers we use, the words we speak, the thoughts we have, are necessary for us, not for God. He sees the heart, and He says, "My child, give me [not your words, but] your heart." In other words, our prayers are an expression of prayer, which consists in love: "The important thing is not to think much [or talk much!] but to love much" (I.C. Mans. IV.1; cf. also ch. 5 of St. Teresa's *Foundations*).

"Seeking my love
I will pass over the mountains
and the river banks;
I will not gather flowers,
nor fear wild beasts;
I will pass by strong men and frontiers."

Commentary

1. Dissatisfied with sighs, tears, and yearnings,
   the soul realizes
   the need of works; the virtues,
   and the spiritual exercises
   of both active and contemplative life.
   Therefore, she must not tolerate
   delights or comforts,
   and must fight
   against the world, the flesh, and the devil.

2. *"Seeking my love"*:
   Not simply with words, signs, etc.,
   but with works; mortifying satisfactions, comforts,
   useless desires.
   Through its own efforts
   the soul must do everything possible;
   cf. the Bride in the Canticle—
   "I will rise . . ." (Cant. 3.1–4).

Theme: Mortification of the natural affections.

(This stanza corresponds to the description in *The Ascent of Mount Carmel* of the Active Night of the Senses, or self-abnegation.)

1–2. Sighs and tears, even acts of love, are not enough. We realize the need for the practice of the virtues, and increased interest in the exercise of the spiritual life. Perhaps for most of us this means greater fidelity and determination to perform these exercises well, and not out of routine. We know also—not only in theory, through having read about it or having heard it from others, but from a conviction borne of our new relationship of love—that anything that is merely a self-indulgence is inconsistent with a genuine desire for God. As St. Teresa never wearies of reminding us, this way we have chosen, this "royal road," is none other than the way of the Cross.

We have to choose one of the two ways, and at this point St. John invites us to make the choice either of settling for a comfortable way of life or of deliberately choosing a more difficult way of "endeavoring to be inclined always 'not to the easiest, but to the most difficult'" (Asc. I.13.6). St. John knows that for most of us, and even for those who have chosen to follow Christ in the religious and the contemplative life, the temptation always remains to seek ways and means of making life more comfortable, of looking for every possible relaxation or indulgence, even while keeping within the framework of a Rule. If the Christian life is the following of Christ, it must be, in its very essence, sacrificial.

"Evangelical perfection" means the acceptance of this as true, and living by it. St. John asks nothing more than the basic demand of the Gospel. In plain terms, what he is saying is: "We shall find happiness when we begin to take the Gospel message seriously." *The Ascent of Mount Carmel* is an elaboration of Luke 14:33: "Unless a man renounces all things that he possesses, he cannot be my disciple." "For," he says, "as long as the soul rejects not all things, it has no capacity to receive the Spirit of God."

1–2. The Saint refers us here, not for the first time, to the Canticle, or Song of Songs. It will be remembered that the poem which

47

3.   Departing from the house
of her own will
and the bed of her own satisfaction,
seeking Him in the day,
not the night,
she will find Divine Wisdom,
the Son of God, her Spouse.

4.   *"I will pass over the mountains
and riverbanks"*:
Mountains, the virtues;
riverbanks, mortifications:
penances, spiritual exercises,
practicing the active
and contemplative life together;
high virtues, lowly mortifications.

he composed (in the prison of Toledo) with a commentary (of which our text is a synopsis) is itself a poetic commentary on the Canticle. Therefore, every reference to the Bible text is of importance, and we will surely make the discovery that St. John's interpretations have a way of lighting up the most difficult passages, when they are seen in the light of our own aspirations for love of God. A thorough study and meditation on each scriptural passage used by the Saint will be immeasurably rewarding.

3–4.   Putting aside all deliberate self-indulgence, and practicing the "high virtues", we inevitably find the Beloved, Christ, the Son of God. What are these "high virtues"? St. Teresa is specific: charity, detachment, humility. "Those who attempt to walk along the way of prayer must of necessity practice [these virtues]" and "Prayer cannot be accompanied by self-indulgence."

The emphasis is not an *acquiring* these virtues, but on the constant, unwearying effort to *practice* them. St. Teresa never equates prayer with the acquiring of virtues but she asserts that prayer must always be accompanied by the courageous, generous effort to practice them. She insists equally, "No virtues [i.e. no honest, determined effort], no prayer life."

The time will come when the effort and the struggle to be virtuous will no longer be needed to the same extent; God comes in to make the practice of virtue seem easy. But we are still in the early stages of our journey; the practice of virtue makes heavy demands, and much effort is necessary.

5.   *"I will not gather flowers"*:
         That is, gratifications, delights—
         temporal, sensory, or spiritual.
         These hinder
         the spiritual nakedness required
         for the narrow way of Christ.
         We need freedom and fortitude
         in seeking Him.
         Ps. 61:11: "If riches abound,
         set not your heart on them."
         Spiritual consolations,
         if possessed or sought with attachment,
         are an obstacle
         to the way of the Cross of Christ,
         the Bridegroom.

6.   *"Nor fear wild beasts;*
         I will pass by strong men and frontiers":
         Wild beasts—the world;
         strong men—the devil;
         frontiers—the flesh.

5.   It goes without saying that self-indulgence of the senses is to
be avoided. What surprises us is the Saint's insistence on not
seeking the "riches" of spiritual consolations, and those things
listed under "goods of heaven" in the Sketch of Mount Carmel:
"glory, joy, knowledge, consolation, rest." "Not these!" he says.
"This way is the way of the imperfect spirit." Even, he says,
when the consolations come from God, even when the visions
or revelations are genuine, we are not to *seek* these things,
with attachment, or wish to possess them; and if they should
occur, we are to attach no importance to them. While they
are in themselves good, not bad, they are no guarantee of virtue
or holiness in the person receiving them, and they easily lead
to presumption. Cf. I.C. I.1.3: "He grants favors of this kind,
not because those who receive them are holier than others";
I.C. VI.8: "No sister should think she is better than the rest
simply because of these favors." Chapters 23–32 of *The Ascent*
deal with this matter: "We should base our love and joy upon
what we neither see nor feel, that is, upon God, who is
incomprehensible and transcendent" (Asc. II.24.9).

6.   Trials from within and without; the Saint is not overstating the
case, but deals realistically with the situation. The "world" has
little understanding and less sympathy for the person genuinely
striving for holiness: good people (even Religious) will discourage those who think of the "higher way" of prayer. St. Teresa
tells us to "resist such people!" The devil will use every means
to prevent progress; the flesh rebels.

7.   The world, "*wild beasts*"— because:
1) It makes her think
       she must live without its favor,
       losing friends,
       reputation, importance, wealth.
2) She is made to wonder
       how she can ever endure
       without the delights
       and comforts of the world.
3) She is made to believe
       that she will be mocked and jeered at.
Hence she has great difficulty
in embarking on
and persevering on this road.

7. St. Teresa, in chapter XXIII of *The Way of Perfection* gives good
    reasons for not turning back once we have set out on the road
    to prayer, "this Divine journey, this royal road to Heaven." She
    constantly stresses the need to be resolute, determined,
    courageous—"for", she says, "people are often timid when they
    have not learned by experience of the Lord's goodness. It is
    a great thing to have experienced what friendship and joy He
    gives to those who walk on this road, and how He takes almost
    the whole cost of it upon Himself."

    St. John of the Cross, the experienced spiritual director, knows
    well what trials can beset us at this time. He is well aware
    that these are temptations; they are very real, but exist often
    in the imagination. "It makes her think"; "she is made to wonder
    how"; "she is made to believe." With God's help, as in every
    case of temptation, they will overcome; but the suggestion is
    that many falter and fall by the wayside for want of a strong
    resolution and reliance on the grace of God. "The time will
    come," St. Teresa tells us, "when we shall realize that all we
    have paid has been nothing at all by comparison with the
    greatness of our prize" (W.P. XXI).

8.   Other "*wild beasts*":
        Interior and spiritual trials,
        temptations of all kinds.

9.   "*Strong men*":
        The devils.
        Their temptations
        are stronger
        than those
        of the world
        and the flesh;
        the devils reinforce their temptations
        with the other two (world and flesh):
        Ps. 53:5: "Strong men
        sought after my soul."
        There is no overcoming the devil
        without prayer, mortification, humility
        (cf. Eph. 6:11–12).

10.   "*Frontiers*":
        The natural rebellion
        of the flesh and the spirit.
        All sensory appetites and natural affections
        must be overthrown.
        Cf. Rom. 8:13: "If by the spirit
        you mortify the flesh,
        you shall live."
        So, required are
        courage and perseverance
        in not stooping to gather flowers;
        strength in passing by
        strong men and frontiers;
        singleness of purpose
        in heading for "the mountains" (virtues).

8–10. Of the three enemies—the world, the flesh, and the devil—
St. John thinks the devil is most to be feared. There is no question
in his mind of the reality of the devil! The devil reinforces his
own strength and cunning by using the enticements of the world
and the flesh to bring us down, especially to discourage us
from going on. St. John is simply re-echoing the warnings of
St. Paul in Ephesians (6:10) that we must use every weapon
in the armory of God in order to defeat him. Against prayer,
mortification, and humility, however, the devil is helpless.
St.Teresa tells us that he will cease troubling the person who
is resolute, and determined to go on courageously (I.C. Mans.
II.1). So we must realize that we have to deal with a strong,
implacable enemy but we must not be afraid; God is on our
side,and we can render the devil powerless by deepening our
faith, by prayer, mortification,and humility. Courage, strength,
singleness of purpose, are needed when the flesh rebels against
the demands of the spirit for detachment: throwing down with
strength and determination "all sensory appetites and natural
affections", lest the spirit should be prevented from going on
to true life and spiritual delight (*text*). Cf. 1 Peter 5:8–10.

"O woods and thickets
planted by the hand of my beloved!
O meadow of green pasture,
enameled bright with flowers,
tell me, has he passed by you?"

Commentary

1.   After self-knowledge,
she begins to walk along the way
of the knowledge of God's creatures.
Cf. Rom. 1:20.

2.   *"Woods"*:
The elements
(earth, water, air, and fire).
"Thickets": their vast number,
their diversity.

3.   *"Planted by the hand"*:
Only God, her Beloved,
could create this diversity and splendor.
Hence, creatures strongly awaken
the soul's love.

4.   *"O meadow of green pasture"*:
The heavens;
their verdure never fades with time.
Cf. also the diversity
of stars and planets.

5, 6.   *"Enameled bright with flowers"*:
Angels; saintly souls
like costly enamel
on a vase of fine gold.

7.   *"Tell me, has he passed by You?"*:
What excellent qualities
has He created in you?

Theme: Knowledge of God in His Creation.

1–4. This joyous stanza corrects any notion we may have that St. John is discouraging us to take any pleasure in the things of the world, God's Creation. The lesson is clear: we have to try to find God there; we are not to be afraid of "the things of the world." This is an important step on the spiritual journey. We are encouraged not to concentrate on ourselves, on our own weakness, brooding over our inadequacy; rather we find food for prayer and meditation in the wonders of God, in His diversity and splendor as seen in the beauty and wonder of His Creation. The sun, the moon, the stars, the sea, animals, plants, birds: everything will remind us of God. The prayerful person will always respond to the beauty of a sunset, the glory of the starlit sky, the delicacy of a tiny flower; the world is always "charged with the grandeur of God" for the prayerful person. At the sight of a running stream, mountains, the green fields, St. John himself would be lost in contemplation. Witness St. Francis of Assisi in this regard. There simply is no question of "attachment" here. The "natural desires" given us by God for the enjoyment of His world are poles apart from the "voluntary desires" for wrongful pleasures. (Chapter 12 of Book I of *The Ascent of Mount Carmel* should be read here.)

5–7. Not only the things about us: we contemplate the angelic hosts as reflecting the glory of God. Furthermore we contemplate ourselves; we ask ourselves the question "What excellent qualities has God given you?" With St. Paul we can say, "By the grace of God I am what I am"; with Our Blessed Lady, "Thanks be to God for the wonderful things He has done in me," both of nature and grace.

"Scattering a thousand graces
he passed by these groves in haste
and looking on them as he went,
with his glance alone
he left them clothed in beauty."

Commentary

1.   The creatures answer the soul;
through His wisdom, the Word,
God created, with ease and brevity,
leaving the trace of Who He is.

2.   *"thousand"*:
That is, numberless.

3.   *"He passed by these groves in haste"*:
"Groves": the elements of nature,
giving them power to generate,
and to conserve in being.
In seeing them,
we see God's grandeur,
His might, and His wisdom.
"In haste": These are the lesser works of God.
The greater are the Incarnation
and the mysteries of faith.

Theme: The grandeur of God as revealed in Creation.

In Stanza 22, paragraph 3, St. John of the Cross, reviewing his commentary on the poem, says of this stanza: "The soul now enters on the contemplative way [or contemplative 'life'], this state continuing until Stanza 12" (S.C.) It should be noted that St. John of the Cross uses the word "contemplation" of that state immediately following discursive meditation (cf. Asc. II.13–16; L.F. 3.32, 33). This is a state of "simple loving awareness, of inner solitude and recollection." It is not to be confused with "infused contemplation" (Stanza 12), which St. Teresa refers to as "supernatural" prayer (compare her "touching on the supernatural," in I.C. Mans. IV.1). When St. Teresa uses the term "contemplation," she, unlike St. John of the Cross, always means "infused" contemplation.

1.   Continuation of the same theme, but now the creatures answer, in one of the most beautiful stanzas of the poem. The stanza contains a profound truth of the theology of Creation: all things were made through the Word "and without Him was made nothing that comes into being" (Jn. 1:3). "Everything comes into being through Him" (Col. 1:15). There is reference here to the Old Testament notion of God's wisdom as personified, accompanying Yahweh in His Creation (Pr. 8.22–36)—as a heavenly being (Sir. 24:1–22) reflecting the majesty and attributes of divinity (Wis. 7:24–8:1), neither identified with Yahweh nor a distinct created being. For St. Paul, "Christ is the wisdom of God" [1 Cor. 1:24].

2–3.   Thus the Word, the Son of God, the Wisdom of God, "in whom are all the treasures of wisdom and knowledge" (Col. 2.3), created in the mere act of "passing by"; not only bringing things into existence with such ease and brevity, in the act of Creation, but in a kind of continuous act of Creation, giving them the power to conserve themselves in being and reproduce their kind.

4.   *"and looking . . . in beauty"*:
Compare Hebrews 1:3: "The Son of God
is the splendor of His glory,
the image of His substance."
He looked at them; that is, through His Son
He gave them natural being,
natural graces and gifts,
in His Word, the Son.
But He also clothed them
with supernatural being
in His Incarnation.
Compare Jn. 12:32:
"If I be lifted up from the earth,
I will draw all things to myself."
Through His Incarnation
and the glory of the Resurrection,
the Father clothed creatures,
beautifying them,
not partially, but wholly.

4. Wonderful as the works of God's material creation are, they are yet the lesser works of God. Greater still is the "new Creation" which results from the Incarnation, Death, Resurrection of Christ. By baptism, we are "plunged into the Paschal Mystery" (Vat. II, *Cons. Liturgy* 6). Having created them in their natural being, God, through His Son, as it were, re-creates them. "O God, who in a marvellous manner didst create and ennoble man's being, and in a manner still more marvellous did renew it" (formerly in the Offertory of the Mass); by baptism, we "share the form of the image of the Son" (Rom. 8:29), who is Himself the "image of the invisible God" (Col. 1:15). The "image of the glory" (2 Cor. 3:18) is to be found ultimately in the Resurrection, through which man "transformed into His image" wears the image of the heavenly man—Christ (1 Cor. 15:49). Therefore, through His Son, the Father beautifies His creatures— not, says St. John of the Cross, in part only, but totally. They are "clothed with supernatural being" in His act of "looking at them."

God made us "partakers of the divine nature." For St. John of the Cross, the total transformation into God, which is the goal of the spiritual journey we have begun, is nothing more than the flowering of the Divine life which was implanted in us in baptism. It is as though a seed (of divine life) is planted in us by God at baptism. We co-operate with the Holy Spirit, and the seed takes root, grows, puts forth branches and leaves, bearing fruit. Through lack of care and nourishment the seed may wither and die. But if we practice the theological virtues of faith, hope, and charity, implanted in us at baptism, we will bring forth abundant fruit.

St. John speaks here of the total union and transformation in God which is possible here below for the soul that is generous in the virtues of the Christian life, who loves God "with his whole heart, his whole soul, this whole being." So, far from being for specialists only, this life (of contemplation) is meant to be for all; it is not the abnormal, but the normal way to God.

Introduction

1.   In contemplative experience,
the loving contemplation of God's creatures
reveals to the soul
something of the infinite supernatural beauty
of the image of God;
"opening His hand, He fills
every animal with blessing" (Ps. 144:16).

Seeing all this visible beauty,
the soul longs
for the invisible beauty of the Creator:

"Ah, who will be able to heal me?
End by wholly surrendering yourself!
Do not send me any more messengers;
they cannot tell me what I wish to hear."

Commentary

2.   Creatures only give signs of the Beloved.
She asks now for His presence,
for total possession of Him,
for sight of Him,
for His total surrender in love.
Communications, traces only of His excellence,
only increase her suffering.

3.   *"Ah, who will be able to heal me?"*:
No worldly delight,
no sensible satisfaction, or spiritual consolation,
can satisfy.

4.   *"End by wholly surrendering yourself!"*:
This is the sign of authentic love—
nothing satisfies except God.
Every glimpse of the Beloved
through knowledge or feeling
increases desire.

Theme: Longing for God's presence; signs do not satisfy.

1. Here, the word "contemplation" does not refer to the "infused contemplation" which will be God's gift and is yet to come. The reflection and meditation—"contemplation" on the beauty of God as seen in His creatures—far from satisfying, causes a loving restlessness, dissatisfaction. These are merely "messengers"; we long, not for the beauty of God's creation, but for the Beauty itself, God himself, "Beauty's self, and Beauty's giver."

2. The demand would seem excessive, presumptuous: the finite asks—demands—the Infinite; nothing less than the total surrender of the Transcendent God to His creature—"End by wholly surrendering yourself!" Only a lover could make such a request; but a true lover can ask for nothing less. God is pleased with our "immense desires," even our importunate demands. If we only knew it, desire is already the possession of Him. Fruition is yet to come.

3–4. Two signs of authentic love of God: the first, that no satisfaction is felt in the worldly things, pleasures, occupations, which previously proved so satisfying. Not only that, even spiritual goods, in which formerly we found satisfaction, now seem distasteful. This is the first of the "signs" given by St. John of the Cross in the ninth chapter of Book II of *The Dark Night* (indicating that the dryness or aridity experienced in prayer at this stage is God's action in the soul to purify it). "The first sign is that we do not get any satisfaction or consolation from the things of God, nor do we get any from creatures, either."

The second sign of authentic love: we feel, we know, that nothing but God will really satisfy us. We go about all our normal activities, but we know, deep down, that "only God suffices."

5.   *All* knowledge of God in this life
       is inadequate, partial, remote.
       The soul asks for essential knowledge.

6.   *"Do not send me any more messengers"*:
       Messengers only redouble
       the sorrow of absence,
       postponing your coming,
       enlarging the wound.

7.   *"They cannot tell me"*:
       Nothing in heaven or earth
       can give the soul
       the knowledge she desires.
       God must be
       both messenger and message.

5. The sublime knowledge of God attained through meditation, or reasoning, or theological study and reflection is but a glimpse of the truth of God—"inadequate, partial, remote from the reality." Cf. Asc. II.8: "It is impossible for the understanding to penetrate into God by means of creatures, be they heavenly or earthly." There must be another knowledge of God, the knowledge which the Holy Spirit—He "who searches the deep things of God" (2 Cor. 2:10)—alone can impart. It is this essential knowledge which we are here asking for in faith, which alone can bring us God Himself, and in love, which emboldens us to make such a demand.

6–7. Yet another "impossible" demand of the lover: no longer will mere intermediaries be welcome (even Angels!). God himself must personally bring His message of love!

"All those who are free
keep telling me a thousand
graceful things of you.
All wound me more,
and a something I know not
that they are stammering
leaves me dying."

Commentary

1.   Formerly, irrational creatures
"wounded" the soul;
now, she is not only wounded
but dying of love,
because of the immensity of God's love
revealed through angels and men,
(rational creatures).

2,3,4.   There are three kinds of suffering:
       1)   being "wounded" (as described) simply.
       2)   being "sorely wounded":
          —from knowledge of the Incarnation,
          —and the mysteries of faith (cf. Cant. 4:19).
       3)   a suffering, festered wound, like death,
          caused by feeling and knowledge of the Divinity.
She is left dying of love
"because she does not die."
This passes quickly.

5,6.   *"All those who are free"*:
That is, angels and men,
in their contemplation of Him.
The angels, through secret inspirations;
men, through instruction
in the truths of Sacred Scripture.

7.   *"a thousand graceful things"*:
The truth of the Incarnation, and the truths of faith.

Theme: Longing for a knowledge of God in His mysteries.

1–4.   We are still, as the Saint says in "The Theme" (p. 16), treating "of the state of beginners." How do we reconcile this with the sentiments of this stanza? We must bear in mind that the time sequence of the poem is by no means precise, and this stanza might well belong to a later stage. "Dying of love" is not an accurate description of the state of soul of a beginner. However, the thought is clear. The more we know of God, especially through instruction, reading, theological reflection, and meditation of the Scriptures, and the mysteries of faith, especially the Incarnation, the more deeply we are affected, wounded; much more so than in the knowledge of God in His Creation. But a third kind of "wounding" is possible, and consists of a fleeting, Divine "touch" in which, in the Saint's words, we have a "feeling and knowledge of the Divinity." This experience is not uncommon, and leaves the person who experiences it inflamed with the desire for God, "dying because she does not die." This is the title of one of St. John of the Cross's best-known poems. This experience, or "feeling," of God's presence passes quickly.

5–7.   Not to be overlooked are the angels; they "teach us interiorly through secret inspiration." Our knowledge comes through the senses; the knowledge of the angels is immediate, infused.

8. *"All wound me more,*
    and a something I know not
    that they are stammering
    leaves me dying."

9. There still remains
    a sublime understanding of God
    to be revealed, inexpressible in words.
    Sometimes advanced souls are favored
    with a sublime knowledge
    by which they have an understanding,
    or experience, of the grandeur of God.
    Then they understand
    that everything remains to be understood.
    It is an understanding of infinitude
    resembling that of the Blessed in Heaven.

10. The experience is indescribable,
    though one may know that it has happened.

8–9.   *"Un no se que"*—in the text, "I don't know what"—might be
       read as "a something which cannot be explained." No matter
       how profound their knowledge, their communications, every-
       thing remains to be said.

       So inadequate is human (and angelic) knowledge of God, that
       St. Thomas Aquinas tells us that every truth we formulate about
       God is, in a sense, an untruth, so incapable are we of expressing
       in human terms the mysteries of God. St. John calls our
       attempting to do this "stammering"; and he reminds us that
       the great favor God gives to some here on earth is that of a
       clear realization that we can never, even in heaven, completely
       understand or experience God. Only the Holy Spirit "searches
       the depths of God" [2 Cor. 2:10]. This observation by the Saint
       (paragraphs 9, 10) is not meant to be applied to those in the
       initial stages—those he is describing in these first twelve
       stanzas.

10.   Common to all mystical experience; we know with certainty
       what has happened, but we can neither explain nor describe
       it without a special gift of God which in itself is a mystical
       grace. Cf. I.C. Mans. V.1: "The soul . . . cannot possibly doubt
       that God has been in it and it has been in God; . . . this certainty
       of the soul is very real, and it can be put there only by God."

"How do you endure,
O life, not living where you live?
the arrows you receive
making you die
from that which you conceive in you
*   of your Beloved?"*

1.   **Introduction**

       Commentary

2.   This life is death, privation of God.
       "Who shall deliver me
       from the body of this death?" (Rom. 7:24).
       The wounds of love
       are enough to end life.

3.   *"How do you endure,*
       O life, not living where you live?":
       Henceforth the soul lives not in the body;
       she gives life to it through love.
       Compare Acts 17:28: "In Him we live . . .";
       Jn. 1:3–4: All that was made . . ."
       The soul's suffering
       arises from two contraries:
       natural life of the body,
       spiritual life in God.

4,5.   *"From that which you conceive . . . of your Beloved"*:
       So impregnated with the touches of love
       which she conceives
       from the grandeur, beauty, wisdom,
       grace, virtues, received from Him.

Theme: Conflict, tension; life as it is in contrast to real life in God, so much desired.

1–5.   Keeping in mind that we are still in the initial stages (because, taken out of context, the impassioned language might mislead us) we arrive now at a point of real conflict; we are drawn strongly in two directions. Our natural inclinations for the good things of this life are still strong, and up to this we gave in to them easily enough; now the love of God draws us even more strongly, and we begin to "live and move and have our being" in Him. Nature rebels, the call of "the world, the flesh, and the devil" persists, and the resulting struggle causes pain and suffering. We look for a way of escape; life seems too burdensome; perhaps only in death can we find the satisfaction we long for. Life seems empty; we long "to be delivered from the body of this death." St. Teresa says: "Everything not of God wearies it, and it knows that it can find no true rest in creatures. [It] seeks a new resting-place, rather than earthly things; and it is here that its suffering really begins" (Mans. V.2).

This longing for life to be ended is not a bad thing, but it is not the sign of great perfection either. The time will come when only what God wants—life or death—will satisfy us. In the meantime this desire for liberation from a world which cannot give us what we know to exist only in God is good and salutary, and a sign of progress.

Introduction

1. Like a wounded stag, the soul,
    wounded by the arrow of love,
    searches this way and that in vain
    for a remedy.
    The stag dies;
    the soul turns finally to God,
    asking that he will slay her
    with the force of love.

    *"Why, since you wounded
    this heart, did you not heal it?
    And, since you stole it from me,
    why did you leave it so,
    not taking off what you have stolen?"*

Commentary

2. Again she asks
    for the healing vision of His presence;
    why has He not come,
    leaving her wounded with love
    coming from knowledge of himself?
    She no longer belongs to herself,
    yet does not belong entirely to God.

3. *"Why . . . heal it?"*:
    That is, slay it completely;
    causing health in the death of love,
    with the delight
    and glory of His presence.

4. *"And, since you stole it from me,
    why do you leave it so . . .?"*
    Stealing her heart,
    without really taking possession.

Theme: Longing to be possessed by God.

1–7.   The conflict and the pain continue, and become more intense. We complain to God: Why, having "wounded" us with the touches of His love, does He delay in giving us Himself? As the stag, wounded, finds solace only in death, so only death can bring to us what alone can "heal"—the presence of the Beloved. We feel ready to be "slain," to give up life itself, for this blessing. Why can it not take place, here and now?

The suffering comes from feeling that God has "stolen" our hearts, without really taking full possession. That is to come; in the meantime, this feeling of emptiness, of being afflicted with an illness for which we see no cure, of being suspended in the air without support, is proof to God that we really love Him. We long for Him alone; no longer are we strongly drawn to worldly things, we find no real satisfaction there. "Love is repaid by love alone".

What is actually happening, in the more technical language of *The Ascent* and *The Dark Night*, is that the purification of the Active Night of the Spirit is taking place and, at this stage, drawing to a close. (It actually ends with Stanza 11.)

5,6.   The two signs of the heart's being truly stolen by God:
its longing for God and
its finding no satisfaction
in anything but Him.
Not fully possessing God,
the soul is like an empty vessel
waiting to be filled;
like a sick person,
moaning for health;
like one suspended in the air
with no support.

7.   *"Not taking off what you have stolen?"*:
Compare Job 7:2–4.

The Theme and Notes 1–7 are repeated here for easy reference.

Theme: Longing to be possessed by God.

1–7. The conflict and the pain continue, and become more intense. We complain to God: Why, having "wounded" us with the touches of His love, does He delay to give us Himself? As the stag, wounded, finds solace only in death, so only death can bring to us what alone can "heal"—the presence of the Beloved. We feel ready to be "slain," to give up life itself, for this blessing. Why can it not take place, here and now?

The suffering comes from feeling that God has "stolen" our hearts, without really taking full possession. That is to come; in the meantime, this feeling of emptiness, of being afflicted with an illness for which we see no cure, of being suspended in the air without support, is proof to God that we really love Him. We long for Him alone; no longer are we strongly drawn to worldly things, we find no real satisfaction there. "Love is repaid by love alone".

What is actually happening, in the more technical language of *The Ascent* and *The Dark Night*, is that purification of the Active Night of the Spirit is taking place and, at this stage, drawing to a close. (It actually ends with Stanza 11.)

Introduction

1.   The soul is like a sick man, tired,
having lost all taste and appetite;
it finds food nauseating,
everything is a disturbance and annoyance.
It has one desire—health.
Therefore, three signs are evident:
longing for health (her Beloved);
loss of taste for all things;
all "things" become burdensome, wearisome.

2.   Seeking only the Beloved
in all her occupations,
and no satisfaction of her own,
like Mary Magdalen in the garden,
everything else becomes a torment:
people, business matters, material concerns.

3.   Compare Cant. 5:6–7: "Those who go about the city"—
that is, worldly people, affairs.
Not only do they not satisfy,
they impede. Hence:

"Assuage these griefs of mine,
since no one else can remove them;
and may my eyes behold you,
because you are their light,
and I would open them to you alone."

Commentary

4,5.   *"Assuage these griefs of mine"*:
Only His Presence can do this.

6.   *"since no one else can remove them"*:
God is very ready
to comfort and satisfy the soul
which has no desires or satisfaction
outside of Him,
and He comes without delay.

7.   *"and may my eyes behold you"*:
That is, face to face, with the eyes of the soul.

Theme: Everything but God is a torment.

1–3.   The "symptoms" described are of one who is "sick"; the distaste
       for the normal good things in life—food, recreation, amuse-
       ments—which formerly gave satisfaction, are, as we said, not
       a sign of perfection; rather a symptom of a kind of sickness.
       The suffering is real, and indicative of God's action in the soul.
       Later, all these activities—people, business matters, material
       concerns—will be viewed in perspective, and, especially when
       they concern the things of God, or where "charity or obedience
       requires it" (cf. St. Teresa, *Foundations*, chapter 5), we will
       come to recognize that they need not be a distraction. We do
       not cease to be less "contemplative" as long as we do not
       become immersed in these activities, to the exclusion of prayer.

       In the words of the Vatican II Document on Religious Life,
       Perfectae Caritatis, paragraph 5, we learn "to combine con-
       templation with apostolic love, seeking God before all things,
       and Him alone." The genuineness of this experience will be
       evidenced by the fact that we center our desires on God in
       a positive way. There is no question of escaping from activity,
       but, as in the case of Mary Magdalen, nothing else really matters
       unless we find Him.

4–7.   Nothing matters now except finding God, the Divine Presence.
       With such good dispositions, St. John assures us that, once
       we have proved that all our desires are centered upon Him
       alone, God not only comes, but comes quickly. There is no
       reason for thinking that the process of our sanctification need
       be long and drawn out; the conditions fulfilled, God acts without
       delay, as we see in the lives of the saints, who in a few short
       years reached the heights, because of singular generosity and
       extraordinary virtue.

8. *"Because you are their light"*:
   Compare Ps. 37:10, Tb. 5:12, Ap. 21:23.

9. *"and I would open them to you alone"*:
   If the soul closes its eyes
   to all things except the light of God alone,
   it merits congruously
   the Divine illumination.

8.   St. John goes on to assure us that, the point of detachment
      having been reached, we actually merit the graces that follow.
      As we shall see later, he places great stress on this point of
      our "meriting" the graces we receive. He uses the technical,
      theological term "*de congruo*": we have no merit in ourselves;
      everything comes from God; but we retain the power to accept
      or reject the grace of co-operating with Him.

9.   The condition once fulfilled, if we so close our eyes to all
      things except the light of God alone, we merit God's gift, meriting
      through the merits of Christ. This is true of our Blessed Lady;
      she, too, "merited" her privileges, but only through the merits
      of her Son. While co-operating in our Redemption, she is the
      first among the redeemed.

Introduction

1.   The affliction of the soul in this state
       causes affliction in the Bridegroom, too;
       compare Zach. 2:8.
       These afflictions touch Him
       "in the apple of His eye."
       Is. 65:24: "Before they call, I will hear . . ."
       Compare Prv. 2:4–5.
       It seems that God
       gives to the soul in this state
       a certain spiritual feeling of His presence
       to increase its fervor
       and prepare it for favors to be granted later.

       "Reveal your presence
       and may the vison of your beauty be my death.
       Behold! Love's sickness has no cure
       except your very presence and your image."

Commentary

2.   Unable to endure her sickness any longer,
       she deliberately asks God
       to show her His beauty—
       His Divine Essence—that, dying,
       she may be freed from this life.
       This, she says,
       is the only cure for her illness.

Theme: If only God would reveal himself!

(This stanza occurs only in the Second Redaction of the poem.)

1.   The suffering intensifies; but God is compassionate. He seems also to suffer, and relieves the pain to a certain extent, giving us a "certain spiritual feeling" of His presence. This "certain spiritual feeling" is not necessarily an "emotional" experience; it is rather a vivid awareness, amounting to a certainty of God's presence with us, around us, in us. It is not a "vision" in the sense that one "sees" Christ. In chapter 27 of the *Life*, St. Teresa explains this: "One day when I was at prayer . . . I saw Christ at my side—or to put it better, I was conscious of Him, for I saw nothing with the eyes of the body or the eyes of the soul. He seemed quite close to me . . . Jesus Christ seemed to be at my side, but . . . I could not see in what form. But I most clearly felt that He was all the time on my right . . . I could not but be aware that He was beside me." She is not speaking of visions, or locutions: ". . . the faculties are not suspended or the senses put to sleep".

2.   Far from consoling us, this rather intensifies the longing. We feel emboldened to ask God to reveal His very beauty to us, so that we might be free of this life: ". . . may the vision of your beauty be my death."

3.   *"Reveal your presence"*:
        God's presence is of three kinds:
        1)   Presence by essence:
        In all created things—a presence by which
        they have life, being, existence.
        This presence is in sinners also.

        2)   Presence by grace:
        God abides in the soul in grace.
        Those in mortal sin lose this.
        No one can know naturally
        that he has it.

        3)   Presence by spiritual affection:
        God grants His spiritual presence
        to devout souls in many ways,
        refreshing, gladdening delighting them.
        But it is a hidden presence.

4.   It is the third presence
        that the soul asks;
        an affective presence, in which
        God grants some semi-clear glimpses
        of His Divine beauty,
        causing ardent desire and longing.
        Ps. 83:3: "My soul longs
        and faints for the courts of the Lord."
        She longs to be engulfed
        in this supreme good,
        which, although hidden,
        communicates a noble experience
        of the good and delight present there.
        She is drawn irresistibly toward it,
        with a force
        far surpassing that of gravity.

3–4. Three kinds of presence of God. A spiritual being is present
not by being "in a place," but wherever it is in operation, or
acting (this is true of God and the angels). Wherever there
is anything in existence, God is there, "operating" to give it
being or keep it in existence. Cf. St. Teresa (i.e. Mans. I.2)
as she insists on this "natural presence" of God everywhere
and in all things, even in the soul which is in mortal sin: "When
the soul falls into mortal sin . . . the Sun himself [God] is still
there in the center of the soul . . . but the soul has no
participation in Him."

The second kind of presence is true of all who are in the state
of friendship with God, or in the state of grace. This is not
limited only to the actually baptized, who have received the
Sacrament. It is true also of all the non-baptized who have
not deliberately separated themselves from grace (e.g. by
deliberate infidelity, apostasy, excommunication). By desire at
least they are "in some way" members of the Church, therefore
united to Christ (cf. *Mystici Corporis* and Vat. II Decree on
Ecumenism, No. 3.) Those of the baptized who commit mortal
sin, but who have not cut themselves off from the Church, remain
members of the Church; but lacking sanctifying grace, they no
longer have the "indwelling" presence of the Blessed Trinity.

The third presence is the one we ask for in this spiritual state—
the presence of God to the contemplative person (who thereby
becomes "contemplative")—in which in a special way God
communicates Himself lovingly to "refresh, gladden, delight";
a kind of glimpse of the divine beauty. It will be understood
that this is what we ask for; it is not given at this stage, but
the very longing for this is a great and precious gift of God.
St. Teresa, in speaking of "the way in which the Spouse awakens
the soul" (I.C. Mans. VI.2) says, "He fills it with fervent desires,
but so delicately that the soul does not understand them." St.
John emphasizes that this presence remains "hidden."

5.   Moses experienced this on Mt. Sinai
      (Ex. 33:12–13):
      "Show me Your face
      that I may know You
      and find before Your eyes,
      the grace which I desire, fulfilled";
      and God answered,
      "You shall not be able to see My face,
      for no man shall see Me and live" (Ex. 33:20).

6.   *"And may the vision of your beauty be my death"*:
      That is, since the delight
      of seeing your being and beauty is unendurable.

7.   The soul does not show outstanding virtue
      in wanting to die;
      for one glimpse of Him,
      a thousand deaths would be desirable.

8.   The soul speaks conditionally,
      supposing that she cannot see God
      without dying.
      To desire death is in itself
      a natural imperfection.

5.　　　Again we must be reminded that what we ask for is not yet given. We come to know of the good we so much desire, and the delights which accompany it, without actually experiencing them. Even Moses could not look on the face of God while in this life; here, perhaps, is the key to understanding the whole doctrinal teaching of St. John of the Cross. The finite cannot see the Infinite; the creature is simply not by nature equipped to gaze on the Creator; He can only communicate through the five senses with the natural world around him. Yet, the creature does arrive at the point of "seeing" God, by a special gift of God. We shall see what this gift is in the next stanza.

6–8.　　Meanwhile we are reminded again that the desire to die and to see God is no sign of extraordinary virtue or perfection. St. John keeps our feet on the ground: "To desire death is a natural imperfection."

"The vision of your beauty ['*hermosura*'] be my death." The Saint speaks again of the "beauty of God" in Stanza 36—"let us go forth to behold ourselves in your beauty" (cf. also Stanza 6). For St. John of the Cross, the beauty of God is the attribute above all which represents the essence of God. Cf. paragraphs 2, 4, and 6 of this stanza, where "beauty" and "being" (the Divine essence) are equated. While others may see goodness, or truth, or love as the highest expression of the divine essence, for St. John, alone among the mystics, the supreme characteristic of God is the Divine harmony of His being, a beauty which is beyond all beauty as we conceive it. In this stanza, we long for the beauty of God; in Stanza 36, we "behold ourselves" in that beauty.

9.   Cf. St. Paul in 2 Cor. 5:4:
        We do not wish
        to be despoiled of the flesh,
        but to be clothed with glory.
        Yet (cf. Phil. 1:23) we desire
        "to be dissolved and to be with Christ."

10.   Unlike the children of Israel,
        for whom death still meant God's absence,
        and who feared
        rather than loved God,
        the soul desires death.
        It is not bitter;
        does not sadden her;
        it is the means to her betrothal and marriage,
        and she longs for it
        above all things.
        Compare Ecclus. 41:3: She knows
        she will be transformed
        into the beauty of God.

11.   "Behold! Love's sickness . . . image."
        Unlike natural illnesses,
        in which contraries are cured by contraries,
        love's sickness is cured
        only by love.
        God alone is the soul's health.

12.   Love is perfect
        only when one lover
        is transformed into the other.
        The soul desires, not the sketch only,
        but the very image of her Bridegroom,
        the Word, the Son of God,
        "the splendor of His glory,
        the Image of His substance" (Heb. 1:3).

13.   Her imperfect love is "sickness";
        she is yet too weak for heroic virtue.

14.   He who feels in himself
        this sickness of love
        should know that this shows
        that he has some love of God.
        Whoever does not feel this sickness
        either has no love
        or is perfect in love.

9–14. St. John points to a certain discrepancy or contradiction in our attitude at this time. On the one hand, we protest that we want to die; on the other, we do not actually wish to leave the body. We are not yet as detached as we think! "To be clothed with glory," yes; but, as St. Teresa wryly observes, "We all want it," implying "Do we all want to make the sacrifices involved?"

Yet, and Saint John presumes this in these passages, the desire for God is stronger than that for the world and the things of the world. Our love, though imperfect, is real, genuine; but it is a "sickness of love"; true, we realize acutely that God alone can satisfy us, that "God alone is our health," but we are "not yet capable of heroic virtue"—not yet, in fact, ready for the Bridegroom.

Yet there is consolation; we will not be discouraged—even to feel this sickness of love, proves that we have some love. Then follows the sobering aphorism: If you do not feel this way, either you don't love God at all, or you are already perfect.

Note: From this point onward, the numbering of the stanzas of this redaction (the second) does not correspond with that of the Saint's first version. Stanza 11, above, is not to be found in the First Redaction. The numbers in brackets after the stanza numbers given here indicate the numbers of corresponding stanzas in the First Redaction—thus Stanza 12 [11].

1.   Calling on God
         to "finish the painting or image,"
         seeing the reflection of God's perfections,
         she turns to faith,
         which contains and hides
         the image and beauty of the Beloved.

         "O Fount so crystal clear,
         if on your silvered face
         you suddenly would form
         those eyes so much desired
         which I hold deep designed within my heart!"

         Commentary

2.   The soul addresses faith,
         as the only means
         to true union, spiritual espousal.
         Compare Hosea 2:19: "I will espouse you to me in faith."
         She asks it to reveal,
         even in obscure knowledge,
         the truths of God,
         by drawing aside the veil (faith).

3.   *"O Fount so crystal clear":*
         Faith is like crystal for two reasons:
         it concerns Christ, the spouse;
         and it is pure in its truth—
         strong, clear, cleansed of error.
         Christ, speaking to the Samaritan woman,
         called faith a "spring," or "fountain,"
         whose waters (the Holy Spirit)
         would leap up to life everlasting
         (Jn. 4:14, 7:39).

Theme: Seeking the Beloved in faith.

1–2.   This is a very important stanza, the last of those which treat of the state of beginners, and the first of the five stanzas. 12–16, dealing with the encounter with God in faith which precedes union. The opening lines correspond to the onset of the Passive Night of the Spirit, to use St. John's terminology. St. Teresa does not use these terms, nor does she emphasize the "darkness" of faith as St. John of the Cross does.

In the conflict described in the previous stanzas, there seemed no remedy except "to be delivered from the body of this death"; now, enlightened by the Holy Spirit, we discover that there is another way. We can find God without dying: we realize that faith will really give Him to us and that it is the only means of achieving true union with Him.

Faith is addressed as a "crystalline fount," or spring. This fountain, faith, at once contains and hides the image and beauty of God. The espousal will really take place; of that we now feel certain, and the meaning of God's word spoken through the prophet becomes clear: "I will espouse [marry] you to myself, in faith."

Not simply: You will learn to believe that I will do this, but you will know (for faith is knowledge) with a certainty begotten of a new kind of "mystical intelligence" which I will give you (faith), so that in knowing, the reality takes place. (Read now St. John of the Cross' poem, "Although 'tis night . . .")

3.   The Holy Spirit is the one leading us to Divine union; His work, His only task, is to bring us to the Spouse, the Risen Christ. It is He of whom Jesus speaks to the Samaritan woman; He who, through His gift of faith, will be "poured forth" like a stream of living water from the Risen Christ, enlivening and enlightening all true believers who henceforth will worship "in spirit and in truth." And from these believers, in turn, fountains of living water flow.

4.   *"if on your silvered face"*:
        That is, in the propositions
        and articles of faith (compared to silver)
        which it teaches us;
        the truth and substance are pure gold,
        which we will enjoy in the next life.
        Compare Ps. 67:14 (faith, the dove;
        its feathers; the truths it tells us).
        So faith gives us God,
        covered with the silver of faith,
        but it gives Him to us *truly*,
        like a gift of a gold vase
        plated with silver (cf. Cant. 1:10).

4.   There seems at first sight to be a contradiction here: faith gives us God, yet it does not give Him. Let us turn to the Saint's own illustration: "If someone were to give us a gold vase plated with silver, he would not fail to give a gold vase merely because it is silver plated." The real gift is the vase made of gold; the fact that we are not aware of its value does not alter the fact that it is ours, ours to possess. The "truth and substance," the pure gold, is God himself. In this kind of living faith, enlivened by love (cf. Gal. 5:6) we do not remain content with formulation of truth—the words in which God's revelation comes to us, important as they are, and absolutely necessary; we want the Person who is Truth, from whom all truth proceeds; God's Revelation to us in His Son, the glorious Risen Christ of here and now. Hence, the insistence of both St. John and St. Teresa on centering our lives and our prayer on the Person of the Risen Christ in His Sacred Humanity—the "pure gold," not merely the outward forms of practices, precepts, devotions, reliance on formulae, or set prayers. All these are important, but secondary. We are reminded of Stanza 1: "She is seeking [the Word] her Bridegroom where the Father feeds in infinite glory" (para. 5). And where is He to be found? He is hidden "by His essence and His presence in the innermost being of the soul" (para. 6).

Cf. *Summa Theologica* II–IIae 11.1: "What appears to be fundamental and the end in every act of believing is the *person* whose assertion is believed; and the things a man assents to are, in a manner, secondary. So the man who has the Christian faith is holding by his will to Christ in matters that are truly part of His teaching." Read Asc. II.3, 4, 9.

5.   *"you suddenly would form*
      those eyes so much desired":
      "The eyes": Divine truths,
      hidden in the articles of faith;
      if only they would give me
      what I desire, completely, clearly, explicitly!
      "Eyes," because she feels
      the great presence of the Beloved.
      He seems always to be looking at her.

6.   *"Which I hold deep designed within my heart!"*:
      "Designed," that is,
      the imperfect knowledge of the Divine truths
      infused into the intellect, by faith.
      When faith gives way to vision,
      we will have the perfect painting (cf. Cor. 13:10).
      "Heart," that is,
      in the soul, in the intellect and will.

7.   Over this design, or outline of faith,
      the outline of love.
      When there is a union of love,
      the Beloved lives in the lover,
      the lover in the Beloved.
      Love produces likeness;
      such is the transformation,
      that each is the other, and both are one.
      Each gives possession of self to the other.
      Each lives in the other.

8.   Compare St. Paul: "I live, now not I,
      but Christ lives in me" (Gal. 2:20)—
      that is, his life was more divine than human.
      Even though, on this earth,
      the soul should experience
      the Spiritual Marriage,
      the transformation is a sketch, imperfect
      by comparison with what is to come.
      Compare Cant. 8:6: "Put me as a seal
      upon your heart."
      The "seal" is the sketch of faith.

5–6.   The Saint distinguishes clearly between "articles of faith" and "Divine truths." He speaks of the "truths *of* the Beloved," the truths *of* God," not the truths *about* God. Seemingly a small point, it is all important to the understanding of the mind of St. John. The Divine truths are Truth Itself. At times there is an overwhelming sense of God's presence ("*por la grande presencia que del Amado siente*"), although in darkness. We know, we "feel," without seeing; God is very near. As St. Teresa reminds us, "He never takes His eyes off you." Note St. John's expression: "He seems always to be looking at her."

   The virtues are infused into the soul at baptism; St. John says "heart", rather than "soul" and explains: " . . . that is, in the soul, in the intellect and will." We will defer discussion of this until we come to Stanza 17.

7.   For the first time we are allowed a glimpse of the astonishing intimacy to which we, in love, are aspiring. For the first time we grasp the meaning of love, its power with God. We see the meaning of St. Thomas' saying, "Love equalizes." Love produces likeness; the lovers are so transformed one into the other that "each is the other and both are one." We recall Our Lord's words: "I am the vine, you are the branches. He who lives in me, and I in him . . ." (Jn. 15:5). "God is love, and he who abides in love abides in God, and God abides in him" (1 Jn. 4:16). As always, St. John of the Cross is "the echo of the Gospel." However, the Saint is anticipating; the transformation in love that he describes is yet to come.

8.   This paragraph should not be taken as describing this particular stage of the journey (note the opening sentence of the next paragraph.) Rather St. John is again anticipating; the transformation is yet to come. We are made aware of the goal, of what we can hope for. St. Teresa uses St. Paul's words—"For me to live is Christ"—to describe the total union of Spiritual Marriage (I.C. Mans. VII.2). St. John reaffirms the point made so often in this work: even should we be brought to the heights of Spiritual Marriage, it is still imperfect in comparison with the union to come, in Heaven; yet it is still a very great blessing.

9.   The soul at this time
        seems like one dying of thirst.
        Compare Ps. 41:2–3: "As the hart
        pants for the living waters . . .";
        it is a thirst which exhausts her,
        and she would pass
        through the afflictions of hell
        if her desires for love could be realized
        (Cant. 8:6, Jb. 3:24).

9.   This paragraph and the introduction to Stanza 13 are a description of the sufferings endured in the Passive Night of the Spirit (refer D.C. II.4–10). Note that the emphasis in both works is different: in *The Dark Night* we have a detailed description of the actual sufferings; in *The Spiritual Canticle* we find emphasis on the reason for the suffering—the object of her desire comes into sight, draws close, and yet is denied her. God, whom she loves, is "intolerable darkness" when He is spiritually near (Stanza 13).

DIVISION II

THE SPIRITUAL ESPOUSAL

Introduction

1.   The soul suffers intensely;
she is drawing nearer to God,
and she experiences the void
of not having God.
She is in darkness;
a spiritual fire dries her up,
purging her;
thus she is purified
in order to be united to Him.
In as much as God does not communicate
some supernatural light,
He is intolerable darkness when He is near.
The supernatural light
darkens with its excess
the natural light.
Compare Ps. 96:2–3: "Clouds and darkness
are around about Him,
fire goes before Him."
Compare Ps. 17:12–13: "He made darkness
His cover and hiding place."
In the measure of her darkness and trial
God grants the soul
favors and consolations,
which at once weary and humble her,
and exalt her.
She seems to go out of her senses.

"Away with them, Beloved,
for I am taking flight!"
(The spouse replies):
"Come back, my dove;
the wounded stag
appears upon the hill
Refreshed in the breeze of your flight."

Theme: Suffering—the Passive Night of the Spirit—God's seeming absence.

1. With this stanza begins the second section of the poem. St. John says these stanzas "deal with the state of proficients in which the spiritual espousal is effected, that is, of the illuminative way." We know, though, that the Saint did not observe a strict time sequence in the poem. Often, as we have seen, he anticipates, treating of a particular state or experience in advance, so to speak. This occurs here. Just as the first stanza was a kind of résumé in advance of the first twelve stanzas, so this stanza describes the experience which in fact is treated in the second division, Stanzas 13–21.

    It deals specifically, then, with spiritual espousal. The tone of the poem changes; a different atmosphere pervades; anxious search gives way to the joy of discovery, meeting, encounter. All this along with greatly intensified suffering, but now God grants also favors and consolation; "She seems to go out of her senses."

    Note that the Passive Night of the Senses, as described in *The Dark Night* (ch. 9 *et seq.*) seems to be omitted in *The Spiritual Canticle*. There is a sudden transition from the Active Night of the Senses, stanzas 1–12 (or more particularly 3–12), to the Passive Night of the Spirit (Stanzas 13–21); these stanzas also correspond to the Fifth and Sixth Mansions of *The Interior Castle*.

    Despite the fact that St. John of the Cross divided the stanzas according to the traditional Three Ways of the spiritual life (see "The Theme," (p. 16) it must be said that for him the really vital points of spiritual progress lay not in these ways (purgative, illuminative, unitive) but in the Nights, or crisis points—that is, in God's direct action on the soul living by faith to purify and detach it. This tallies with our own personal experience and daily living. We ordinarily live in darkness— in the 'Night' of the obscurity but certainty of faith all our lives. This way of faith is to be desired and preferred.

Commentary

2.   So sublime is the chaste
        and delicate revelation of the Beloved
        that the soul
        is carried out of herself
        in rapture and ecstasy,
        which causes great suffering
        in the sensory part.
        Unable to endure it,
        she says *"Away with them, Beloved"*—
        that is, your Divine eyes—
        for they cause me to take flight
        and go out of myself
        in highest contemplation,
        and the body cannot endure it.

3.   *"Away with them, Beloved"*:
        Such is the misery of the human nature,
        unable to endure
        what it desires so ardently.

2–3.   The question arises: If, then, we do not experience these things which are now described, such as raptures and ecstasy, what is the use of thinking of the "higher way", of infused contemplation? Do only "contemplatives" experience these things? If we read St. John of the Cross and St. Teresa superficially we might think so; they seem to be saying "At this stage, this will happen." Yes, but not inevitably and in every case; one might say, not even in the majority of cases. These raptures may occur, and our Saints have written to instruct people regarding their relative importance, their value, and how to recognize that they are genuine, and from God. St. John also has directors of souls in mind, enabling them to advise people who have these experiences.

But God can, and does, give consolation in another, less spectacular way—the deep, peaceful joy in the midst of suffering, a joy which in itself is a grace, a gift from God.

St. Thérèse of Lisieux is an example of this. No one ever saw her in "rapture" or "ecstasy." In the midst of deep suffering, she could say, "I know Jesus is there, in my heart; I do not see Him." In any case, both saints, St. Teresa and St. John of the Cross, insist that rapture and ecstasy, far from necessarily indicating holiness, are a sign of the person's weakness to bear the nearness of God (cf. I.C. Mans VI, 7; VI, 8; VI, 9; cf. paragraph 4, following).

4.   The suffering arises
        from the body's being unable
        to receive such favors,
        which are a communing of spirit
        with the Divine Spirit
        coming to the soul.
        The soul must then in some way
        abandon the body; it being a unity,
        this separation causes pain,
        added to that of the fear
        of awareness of the supernatural.

5.   The soul
        does not really want God to withdraw;
        on the contrary,
        she wishes to take flight, as it were,
        outside the body,
        to rejoice freely in the Beloved.

6.   "*I am taking flight*":
        The spirit of the soul
        is carried away violently;
        it ceases to have its feelings and actions
        in itself,
        since it has them in God.
        Compare Cor. 12:2: "In the body,
        or out of the body, I know not . . ."
        This is rapture experienced by those
        who have not yet reached the stage of perfection;
        they are called "proficients."
        The perfect receive all communications
        in peace and gentle love.
        Raptures such as this cease—
        they are only preparatory
        to the reception of total communication.

4–6.   The body is unable to bear this experience of the spirit
        communing with the Divine Spirit; by nature it is not equipped
        for this inflow of the supernatural. A gradual "spiritualization"
        of the person is taking place and in the beginning, the body,
        unable to adapt readily, rebels, as it were, and the conflict
        between spirit and body is painful. Cf. Stanza 40.5: ". . . the
        bodily senses which are . . . purified and spiritualized " (in
        Spiritual Marriage).

        St. Teresa describes this state in chapter XX of *The Life*: "The
        Lord gathers up the soul . . . as the clouds gather up the vapors
        from the earth, and raises it up til it is right out of itself, and
        the cloud rises to heaven and takes the soul with it." With
        St. John, she speaks also of "the terrible fear" felt; but a fear
        "overpowered by the deepest love." The effect on the soul is
        a "strange detachment" which is also, in some mysterious way,
        shared by the body, so that life seems "more distressing." Not
        to be overlooked is the fear caused by the nearness, and new
        awareness, of the supernatural.

        Again, we are reminded by St. John that this is but a stage
        of the journey, to be passed through; we do not linger here
        (if God has given us this experience). The conflict and suffering
        are a sign of imperfection, weakness; "the perfect receive all
        communications in peace and gentle love." Yet, lest we under-
        estimate God's action and intention in giving this experience,
        we are reminded by St. Teresa that the benefits to the soul
        are very great: " . . . it distinctly recognizes the very great benefit
        which each of these raptures brings with it"—notably a new
        detachment and freedom "so that it cannot recognize itself."

7.   This would be the place
        for describing in more detail
        such raptures, ecstasies,
        and elevations of the soul.
        This is unnecessary,
        as the blessed Teresa, our Mother,
        left writings about these spiritual matters,
        which are admirably done.

8.   *"Come back, my dove"*:
        The time has not yet come
        for the lofty contemplation
        in which you aim
        after true possession of me;
        adapt yourself to this rapture,
        this lower knowledge of Me.

9.   *"The wounded stag"*:
        That is, the Bridegroom,
        also feels the wound of the Beloved,
        as a stag seeking out and sharing
        the suffering of its wounded mate.

10.   *"appears upon the hill"*:
        That is,
        like the stag, which seeks high places.
        He says he "appears on the hill"
        of the loftiest contemplation;
        the "high place"
        where God begins to communciate himself
        in this life,
        is like a glimpse of God from a distance.

7–10.   Neither St. John nor St. Teresa makes any sharp distinction
        between rapture and ecstasy. We know that both Saints experi-
        enced them, and both speak from personal experience. Their
        teaching is substantially the same—that rapture, ecstasy, "flight
        of the spirit" (as St. Teresa terms one kind of rapture) are,
        despite their "spectacular" appearance, not to be confused with
        holiness, and are a "lower form" of knowledge of God, despite
        their value to the person experiencing them.

        They are accompanied by much suffering, and the person
        usually asks God to take them away, as they attract the attention
        and often the harsh criticism of others, especially one's
        confessor, if he fails to understand. St. Teresa is at pains to
        remind such a person not to think that true holiness has been
        achieved because of these favors; cf. I. C.Mans VI.6.

        In *The Interior Castle*, after devoting chapters 4, 5, and 6 of
        the Sixth Mansion to describing raptures and ecstasies, she
        writes a chapter on "the importance of keeping in mind the
        Sacred Humanity of Christ," lest, as she says, "these souls will
        now be so sure of themselves that they need not fear or weep
        for their sins." And "if she loses her guide, the Good Jesus,
        she will be unable to find the Way." There follows very practical
        advice on how to pray and even how to practice meditation
        at this stage.

        St. John reminds us that the Bridegroom continues to share
        the suffering as well as the joy at this time, and tells the bride
        (we, ourselves, who have come thus far) to have courage.
        Though we cannot see the goal, He already sees it; the heights
        ("hill") of the loftiest contemplation.

11.   *"refreshed in the breeze of your flight"*:
         "flight" means contemplation;
         "breeze", the spirit of love—
         the Holy Spirit, who is Love,
         the "breath" of the Father and the Son.
         Note, by the breeze of your flight—
         not by contemplation,
         considered as knowledge of God
         in His mysteries,
         but through the love
         arising from this knowledge.
         For just as love
         is the union of the Father and the Son,
         so it is union of the soul with God.
         Compare 1 Cor. 13:2 and Col. 3:14:
         "Charity, the bond of perfection."

11. Paragraph 11 is of the utmost importance. It brings into relief
that which is most characteristic in the Carmelite view of
contemplation: love, as well as knowledge, but especially love.
Insofar as contemplation is considered as knowledge of God
and His mysteries, and that alone, it will not bring about union
with God; but the knowledge which finds its completion and
culmination in love—it is this which unites.

So while the classic definition of contemplation, "simple gazing
on Truth," is, rightly understood, correct, St. John, and the
Carmelite spiritual writers, would add "with love." "Contemplation is knowledge and love together, that is, loving
knowledge . . ." (L.F. 3.32). God communicates himself ". . .
through the love arising from knowledge of Him" (*text*).
Knowledge causes love, and love is the reason for God's
communication of a more profound knowledge of himself.

The Spirit of union, the uniting principle, He who promotes
and brings about the union of the soul and God, is the Holy
Spirit, who is Love itself, Love in Person. This is His function,
His task: to bring us to Christ, the Bridegroom. "The love of
God is poured forth in your hearts by the Holy Spirit" (Rom.
5:5); "love, which binds together in perfect harmony" (Col.
3:14.) It is through this contemplation (infused, or "poured
in," by the Holy Spirit) uniting us to the Risen Christ and to
the Father that we will be brought into that direct, intimate,
loving relationship with God which is infused contemplation.

12.   Love is a flame, that burns
with a desire to burn more.
One love enkindles another.
God does not give grace and love
except according to the soul's desire and love.
The more the soul desires and loves,
the more God gives.
How is this love to be acquired?
The answer is in St. Paul, 1 Cor. 13:4–7:
"Charity is patient, kind . . . endures
all things."

12.   The soul that truly loves God is filled with longing for greater love. "It becomes restless with desires"; "Her desires become so-great as to cause her great distress" (I.C. Mans. V.2; VI.11). Cf. Also I.C. Mans. VI.2: "He fills [the soul] with fervent desires, but so delicately that the soul does not understand them." Also Mans. VI.11: "The more the soul learns about the greatness and goodness of God, the more her desire increases." In a sense, it is true that the desire for the love of God is already the accomplishment; the good desires come from God, and as St. Thérèse of Lisieux reminds us, "God would not give such desires for love of Him if He did not intend to fulfill them." She speaks in her Act of Oblation of her "infinite desires." St. John says that God gives grace and love in accordance with our desires.

To keep our feet on the ground, lest we should be lost in our beautiful thoughts about love, St. John gives us a sobering reminder: this love is acquired by practicing charity towards our neighbor. It is all in the thirteenth chapter to the Corinthians; St. Paul tells us that the way to God is not that of the wonderful gifts of prophecy, tongues, or miracles: "I will show you," he says, "a more excellent way." In *The Interior Castle* (Mans. V.3), St. Teresa says that if we "lack charity concerning our neighbors," we are "far from attaining union with the will of God." That, she says, is the only union she really wants for us, not the union of "absorption." "I sought God, He had withdrawn from me; I sought my soul, and could not find it; I sought my neighbor, and found all three."

Introduction

1.   Compare Gen. 8:9: "Return, dove . . .";
Noah in his compassion
caught the returning dove,
placing it in the ark (of charity).
The soul sings of the grandeur of the Beloved:

"My Beloved; the mountains,
the lonely wooded valleys,
the strange islands,
the resounding streams,
the whisper of love-laden airs.

The night serene,
the time of rising dawn,
the silent music,
the souling solitude,
the supper which refreshes and increases love."

2.   These two stanzas
describe the beginning of the state
called spiritual espousal—
with the Word, the Son of God—in which
God communciates to His bride
great things about Himself,
adorns her with gifts and virtues,
clothing her with knowledge of Himself,
as a bride is adorned.
On that day,
her vehement complaints cease;
there begins a state of peace, delight, gentleness.
In the remaining stanzas,
no longer does she speak
of sufferings and longings
as she did before,
but of the communion and exchange
of sweet and peaceful love;
because all those other sufferings
have ceased.

Theme: Joy follows suffering: beginning of the spiritual espousal; communion and exchange of love.

1-2.   Our first impression on reading these two stanzas, and the commentary, is that from now on all will be sweetness and light; sufferings will end. Like Peter, we may exclaim: "Lord, it is good for us to be here"; and we would like to remain with the glory of it all.

Yes, there is much joy; we are now able to sing, in the gladness of our new discovery of God's love, of His greatness, of His beauty, of His Divine attributes, which before we understood so imperfectly. God begins to communicate to us "great things about Himself," and—note this line well—"adorns her with gifts and virtues." Something *new* is beginning!

We begin to realize that it is not so much "practicing virtue," as before; from now on God communicates something of Himself. The practice of virtue seems easier, and our virtues seem no longer ours, but God's, so there is no room for complacency. Cf. I.C. Mans. V.2: "God impresses something of Himself on the soul." God "clothes her with knowledge of Himself." We begin to understand the "Magnificat": "Blessed is He who has done great things in me." The bride is being adorned by the Bridegroom, and she realizes that the beautiful adornments are His, not hers. But she wears them with grace and dignity! Jesus' words in the Gospel now have a deeper meaning: "Learn of me, because I am gentle and humble of heart." In humility, we begin to "walk in truth."

These stanzas describe the highest graces
that God communicates to the soul
at this time; not all souls
experience everything described here.
To some is given more,
and to others, less.

3.   The bosom of God
        is compared to the Ark,
        in which there were many rooms
        and all kinds of food (Gen. 6:14–21).
        The soul finds "many mansions"
        in her Father's house (Jn. 14:2).

4.   The soul finds here
        all the rest, recreation, abundance, and riches
        she could desire. She understands
        secret and wonderful knowledge of God,
        discovering in herself
        the power and strength of God.
        She finds spiritual sweetness and delight,
        true quiet, Divine light,
        and tastes of the wisdom of God
        reflected in His creatures and works.
        She is filled with blessings
        and emptied of evil.

3–4   "No longer does she speak of sufferings . . . all those other sufferings have ceased" (*text*). One must study the wording very carefully in order to arrive at the Saint's meaning. Let us not hastily conclude that all suffering has ceased. "She no longer speaks of sufferings . . . [in the remaining stanzas] as she did before . . . all those other sufferings have ceased." All this will be clarified by the Saint in the last paragraph (paragraph 30) of the commentary on these two stanzas.

Suffice to say here that there is still much suffering, but our attitude toward it has changed. Cf. I.C. Mans. VI.11: "The soul feels the pain to be so precious that . . . it suffers it very gladly . . ."God is giving us something of Himself, and that means He is imparting to us something of His own understanding of the meaning of suffering in our lives, as Jesus understood it in His.

This is a very precious grace, and the key, in a sense, to the spiritual life. No longer are we preoccupied with our own suffering, complaining of God's absence, our own pain and crosses. We are now more preoccupied with the "communion and exchange of sweet and peaceful love," sweetness and peace which is now possible along with (not despite) the suffering of the absence of God. This is still very real, but the intermittent "touches" of God are experienced in a manner which brings this new peace and joy, the bliss of union, which, as St. Teresa says, "is nothing else than two different things becoming one." We "discover in ourselves the power and strength of God."

5. The soul knows the truth
of St. Francis' saying,
"My God and my All."
She experiences
a strong, overwhelming communication,
a glimpse of what God is in himself.
God is all things for her.
All that is explained in the stanzas
applies to God
eminently and infinitely.

6. *"My Beloved; the mountains"*:
That is, vast, like the mountains,
with lush foliage, graceful, fragrant.

7. *"the lonely wooded valleys"*:
In solitude and silence,
giving refreshment and rest
in cool shades.

8. *"strange islands"*:
God is far removed
from men and angels.
The soul discovers its own incapability
of seeing or understanding God,
in himself,
or in His ways and dealings with His creatures.

5–8.   We have been reminded by the Saint that not all of us will experience all that he describes. This is what *may* be experienced at this time. There is an overwhelming sense of God, as never before. Previously (Stanzas 4, 5, 6) we discover God *in* all things of Creation. Now, mysteriously, He *is* all things. But this is not pantheism; it is rather the felt experience of a theological truth regarding the nature of God.

We can truly say, God *is* Wisdom, He *is* Truth; "God *is* Love." (1 Jn. 4:16). St. Francis' prayer is better rendered: "My God, and all things [to me]" ["*Deus Meus, et omnia*"]. St. John says, "*Dios mio y todas las cosas*." (Cf. Stanza 37.7.)

Explaining St. John's use of the theological terms "eminently and infinitely," as simply as possible, we may say that if we could think of any virtue, or perfection, such as goodness, love, wisdom, truth, existing in all perfection, in this world, in human beings, and containing all possible imaginable perfection, that would be only the taking-off point for our understanding of the perfection of these virtues in God, in whom all goodness has its being. The perfection of virtue in man is still finite, limited; virtue in God, insofar as we can apply that term to Him, is infinite, without end.

Holiness in man is but a sharing in the holiness of God. The study of theology teaches this; here we discover it by experience, "mystically" (we mustn't be afraid of the word). We discover the truth that "we are incapable of seeing or understanding God, in Himself, or in His ways and dealings with His creatures." It is the grace of knowing that we cannot know, of ourselves.

Now perhaps we can see why St. John says, "My beloved [is] the mountains . . . the valleys, the strange islands." Previously they were "messengers," "signs" of God. (Stanza 6); now all things are, in a certain way, identified with Him, in the sense that we see Him in them.

9.   *"the resounding streams"*:
        The Divine onslaught
        is like the overwhelming force
        of a river in flood, engulfing the soul,
        drowning all her former actions and passions.
        She does not regret this;
        these rivers are rivers of peace,
        despite the force of their floodwaters.
        Compare Is. 66:12. "I will descend
        and besiege her like a river of peace,
        like a torrent overflowing with glory."

10.   *"Resounding"*:
        That is, a loud cry or call;
        the spiritual, interior voice
        similar to that of the Holy Spirit
        coming to the Apostles like a mighty wind.
        Cf. Jn. 12:27–29: The Jews
        heard the voice of the Father to Jesus
        as thunder; or as an angel from heaven,
        denoting the fortitude
        interiorly bestowed on Christ (cf. Apoc. 1:15).
        Cf. Ps 67:34: "God will give to his voice
        the sound of power."

9   There is a suddenness, a power, in God's coming. St. John says it is a "divine onslaught' (*este embestir divino*); St. Teresa says, "It is like a great flood tide released by God to sweep the soul on high" (I.C. Mans. VI.5). And, wonderful to relate, "drowning all her former actions and passions" (*text*). Here we are confronted with this altogether new element in our spiritual lives: a kind of invasion of God, "taking over" our whole being in such a way that we are purified of the miseries and weakness which formerly beset us. Strangely enough, along with this realization of being purified by God, there remains an ever-increasing sense of one's own worthlessness, sinfulness. St. Teresa says: "The result of this action of God is that the soul realizes its own foolishness, and the worthlessness of its own good actions" (i.e. Mans. VI.5). And although the experience is overwhelming, it brings with it deep peace—"like a river of peace" (Is.66:12), which is at the same time like a river in flood!

10.   St. John likens this, by way of explanation of an apparent con-tradiction, to the gentle breeze of the Holy Spirit, which was like a mighty wind on Pentecost Day, and to the voice of the Father, coming gently, interiorly to Jesus, but sounding like thunder to the bystanders. He implies that we, too, are interiorly strengthened by God, with the fortitude needed to bear the nearness of God's presence. In the same chapter of *The Interior Castle*, St. Teresa reminds us that "the soul is at first filled with fear, and great courage is necessary to bear it."

11.   Cf. Apoc. 14:2: "Like the voice of many waters
        and like the voice of a great thunder";
        so gentle, too,
        "like many playing on harps."
        As God speaks to the bride in the Canticle:
        "Let your voice sound in my ears,
        for your voice is sweet" (Cant. 2:14).

12.   "*the whisper of love-laden airs*":
        That is, the delight of the soul
        in the knowledge of the attributes of God,
        overflowing in the intellect,
        producing knowledge and feeling of delight.

11.   There is a gentleness in God's dealings with us. He knows our weakness, and in the paragraphs which follow we can almost feel the reminiscence of a lover—St. John himself—calling to mind how gently, lovingly, God first reveals Himself. This is the joy of the one who, having fallen in love, discovers that the loved one has good qualities and perfections undreamed of. Here it happens that we accept the Beloved because of love alone, only to discover that He is perfect and that those perfections—His goodness, His loveliness—are infinite, inexhaustible. This new knowledge, (formerly known theoretically, by hearing and reflection) now becomes a reality lived, felt, experienced; it is still, and always will be, knowledge in faith; but the intellect is enlightened so that the new knowledge produces a "feeling of delight".

12.   Regarding this "knowledge and feeling of delight" which is experienced: the order seems to us reversed. We ordinarily expect that pleasure, or consolation, will be felt in the senses, received in the intellect and the will, and enjoyed in the soul. That is the normal way of acquiring knowledge, and therefore of having pleasurable experience. Here, though, the soul is "touched" directly by God, who imparts knowledge of Himself, without images or concepts. The joy overflows into the intellect, producing knowledge of God and His mysteries and attributes, acquired without learning; with it, great consolation. This is what St. Teresa calls "spiritual consolation," as opposed to ordinary "sweetness" in prayer. "Spiritual consolations, however, have their source in God, even though they may bring us natural joy and satisfaction" (I.C. Mans. IV.1). This kind of spiritual consolation "enlarges the heart" (Ps. 118). See also I.C. Mans. IV.2.

13.   The sentiment of the Beloved's attributes
         is felt and enjoyed
         by the soul's power of touch,
         which is in its substance,
         and the knowledge of them
         is felt and enjoyed
         in the intellect.

14.   The touches are "love-laden airs,"
         "whispering" or penetrating sweetly
         into the inner substance of the soul.
         The intellect receives the knowledge
         without any efforts of its own,
         that is, passively.
         Compare Elias: "whistling of the gentle breeze"
         (3 Kgs. 19:11–13).

15.   This Divine "whisper" implies
         not only the understanding of the truths of faith
         but also
         an unveiling of truths about the divinity
         and a revelation
         of the secrets of God—pure spiritual revelations
         without the help of the senses.
         It is a communication of God
         through "hearing" in a spiritual way,
         whereas the ordinary truths of faith
         come through hearing,
         which implies assent of the understanding,
         that is, seeing with the eyes of the passive intellect.
         Cf. St. Paul, who heard secret words
         "which men are not permitted to utter"
         (2 Cor. 12:4). Compare also Job 42:5.

16.   This knowledge is not the perfect
         and clear fruition of heaven.
         In this life,
         contemplation is a ray of darkness.

17–21. Commentary on Job 4:12–16.

13–16. Since St. John uses the terms "substance" of the soul and "understood substance" so frequently, we must remember that this is a communication of "substance to substance." God communicates himself, in His very being (substance) to the very being (substance) of the soul, or person, and this without any intermediary. God "bypasses" the ordinary means of communication—senses, intellect, and will—to "touch" directly, substantially, the innermost sanctuary of soul. These divine touches are spiritual revelations of the secrets of God without the help of the senses. Cf. I.C. Mans. VI.4: "The soul . . . has never before had such light and knowledge of God . . . it is able to apprehend supernatural truths according to God's pleasure in revealing them."

The words "seeing with the eyes of the passive intellect" must be interpreted in the light of the difficulties the Saint has in using ordinary terms to explain what he termed, in the Prologue, the "unexplainable." In fact, nothing is "seen" or "felt" in the ordinary way; the characteristic note of these substantial touches is that they are, to use the Saint's terminology again, "stripped bare" ("*desnudas*") of all forms or images perceptible to the senses.

That the soul in its very being, or substance, can in any way lay hold of the reality which is the very being, or substance, of God is altogether an exceptional gift of God. It is a sign that we have really come to the point of desiring, once and for all, complete self-surrender to God and that, through our co-operation with grace, we have been purified of all unmortified, disorderly attachments of the senses and the appetites.

17–21. This summarizes the teachings of Stanzas 12–15.

22.   *"The night serene"*:
        In this spiritual sleep
        the soul possesses
        and relishes tranquillity, rest, and peace
        in this fathomless, obscure, Divine knowledge.

23.   *"the time of rising dawn"*:
        Not like that of a dark night,
        but rising dawn of Divine light;
        from the darkness of natural knowledge
        to the morning light
        of supernatural knowledge.
        This light is still obscure.

24.   Cf. Ps.101:8: "I have kept watch
        and am become
        like a solitary sparrow on the housetop."
        The sparrow perches at a height,
        that is, perfect contemplation.
        It turns into the wind,
        that is, toward the spirit of Love, who is God.
        It is usually alone,
        it sings sweetly (in praise of God);
        it has no definite color,
        that is, no sensible affection or self-love.

25.   *"silent music"*:
        God's creatures and works
        now reveal Him
        in tranquillity and silent knowledge
        of the Beloved.
        He is the silent music, and—

26.   *"the sounding solitude"*:
        Compare John in Apoc. 14:2—
        that is, "silent" to the natural senses,
        but resounding
        in the spiritual faculties,
        emptied of all natural forms, apprehensions.
        God is revealed in himself
        and in His creatures.

22–23. Whatever we may suffer naturally in this experience of God's nearness, in another way there is an experience of deep, lasting peace which no suffering of daily life can disturb. Not that the knowledge of God is clear, distinct; it remains obscure. But as we see in Number 23, it is obscurity of a different kind from that previously known in the purification of the Dark Night. Now there is darkness, but darkness illumined by the light of dawn. The "morning light," still somewhat obscure, brings with it the certainty that day is dawning.

24–26. For now, the Saint assures us, we have entered the realm of "perfect contemplation." Not that everything has yet been given, or achieved; but we have entered, crossed the threshold. Like the sparrow on the housetop in Psalm 101, we experience a new kind of solitude (not loneliness, quite the contrary); we are content, and prefer to be alone with God, though that does not make us neglectful of our duty, the daily task; there is a new orientation in our lives; we are habitually turned toward the spirit of Love; a new note is heard in our prayerful utterances, the note of praise of God. There follows a delectable desire to enjoy Him and the soul makes many acts of praise to the Lord (cf. I.C. Mans. VI.2). Self-love, disordered affection for anything not of God, is out of the question.

Everything speaks of God, and the beauty of Creation is appreciated in a new way (cf. Stanzas 4, 5). Previously, God was *in* His Creation; now He *is* the silent music, the "sound in silence," relished in silent, wordless adoration. Before, God spoke in signs; now He speaks in silence. "And they sang a new song . . . as they heard a voice from heaven like the sound of many waters" (Apoc. 14:2).

27.   The soul recognizes
        that all God's creatures,
        bearing God within themselves
        in their own way,
        raise their voices to glorify God.
        Cf. Wisdom 1:7: "The Spirit of the Lord
        fills the whole earth,
        having knowledge of His Voice";
        the voice of the "sounding solitude"
        giving glory to God.

28.   *"The supper which refreshes and increases love"*;
        As in Scripture,
        "supper" means the divine vision.
        The end of the day's work;
        the beginning of evening rest.
        God is the supper, refreshing,
        bringing with His presence the end of all evils;
        increasing love, which, to possess,
        is the possession of all that is good.

29.   Cf. Apoc. 3–20: "If anyone opens, I shall enter
        and sup with him and he with me."
        God's delightful "supper" is Himself;
        he graciously share His own goods,
        His own self,
        in the exchange of love.

30.   Let it be noted
        that in this state of espousal
        the tranquillity in the soul
        refers to the superior part.
        The bride still suffers
        from the dross left from bad habits,
        from the withdrawal of the Beloved,
        and from disturbances and afflictions
        in her sensory part, and from the devil.
        All these will cease in the state of Spiritual Marriage.

27.   It is impossible not to be impressed with St. John's sensitivity to God's Creation. In this stanza we not only see God in His Creation; there is also a deeper understanding of His creatures— they "bear God within them," in their own way. It is a bold statement; Teilhard de Chardin is anticipated. Unlike man, made in the image and likeness of God, by grace they yet bear the divine imprint. St. Thomas Aquinas says they bear the "impression of the Divine Wisdom." In their very existence they are a sign of God, and glorify God; only man can glorify God with a positive act of his will. With this new insight into Creation, the thought of God leads us to praise and adoration; we experience a new, mystical awareness of our oneness with all Creation; we become aware, with St. John, of the cosmic significance of the Incarnation. The Word, in whom all things were made, becoming Flesh, ennobled all flesh and all created things. Everything created becomes for us a Sacrament of God.

28–29. The supper is essentially exchange of friendship; sharing; giving: "I shall sup with him, and he with me." Here again we find that the supper is identified with the Beloved; the delightful supper is Himself. We think of the Eucharistic banquet; it is not we who assimilate Christ, but we who are assimilated to Him, the glorious Risen Christ. He is ready, according to our disposition, to communicate himself to us, with all His virtues and perfections. He shares His own goods, himself, with us in this loving exchange, the "admirable exchange" of the Liturgy of the Christmas season. The Eucharist is the sacramental expression of our union with the Beloved; it expresses love, and deepens it, causing new love in the soul.

30.   A clarification of paragraph 2 of the commentary on Stanzas 14, 15, "No longer does she speak of sufferings." Not yet perfect, we suffer from ourselves, especially from our own inadequacy for this union with God. We are not spared the ordinary sufferings of life, and can still be tempted. Nevertheless there is real peace of soul. We know the meaning of joy in suffering. "With the aid of God, suffering becomes easy" (I.C. Mans. VI.4).

Introduction

1.   The soul experiences sublime enjoyment;
conscious of her virtues,
and of habitual peace
in the visits of the Beloved,
she makes the gift of herself,
with all her virtues,
as a bouquet of flowers.

2.   The devil tries
to stir up the sensory appetites,
or to produce a variety of images
in the imagination,
and to cause disturbance
in the spiritual part of the soul.
He esteems it of more value
to upset one such soul
than many others.
Only God can bring tranquillity
in this state;
it is not in the soul's power
to be free of these disturbances (cf. Ps. 33:8).

So, speaking to the angels
whose duty it is to assist her,
she says:

"Drive off those little foxes,
for our vineyard is now in flower,
while we make a pine-like cluster of roses;
and let no one appear on the hill."

Theme: Peace in the nearness of the Beloved; consciousness of virtues, along with sensual temptation.

1–2. The joy we experience in this new life of closeness to God, the habitual peace because of His nearness and frequent visits, along with the consciousness of having acquired virtues which are God's gifts, not the result of our own efforts—all these lead us to an act of total self-giving. But the joy is offset by the sufferings caused by the devil; disturbances of mind, temptation in the form of sensual imagination, beset us. Not that the devil's sole aim is to succeed in tempting us to actual sin; he hopes rather to upset and disturb our serenity and peace of soul.

St. John is very emphatic about the value placed by the devil on one person who is truly detached and humble, and resolute in proceeding on the way to contemplation. One such person is of more value to the Church than many others, and the devil will make any effort to bring about his downfall. Cf. I.C. Mans. V.4: "The devil will . . . use every means to prevent the betrothal . . . will marshall all the powers of hell, for to win one soul like this is to win a whole multitude." I.C. Mans. IV.3: "The devil sets greater store by one soul in this state than by a great number of souls to whom the Lord does not grant these favors." St. John of the Cross believes that the loss of a little "pure gold" is for the devil much worse than the loss of many other "base metals". He says that we seem to be powerless to combat these temptations; God alone can help us. So we turn to Him through His messengers, the angels, asking their aid. We have the humility to recognize that we have an adversary, the devil, much more powerful than we are. But we have a "secret weapon"—humility, rooted in faith, against which the devil is helpless.

Commentary

3.   *"Drive off . . . flower"*:
The vineyard,
the nursery of all the soul's virtues,
produces a sweet-tasting wine.
"in flower": when the soul
is united to the Bridegroom
(cf. Ps. 62:2).

4,5.   *"foxes"*:
Just as foxes
pretend to be asleep
when they are out to catch their prey,
so these sensory appetites and imaginations awaken
when the virtues blossom and flower
in an exercise of love.
Gal. 5:17: "The flesh lusteth against the spirit."
These disturbances are the "foxes."

6.   The demons assail the soul in two ways,
inciting the appetites and the imagination,
assailing her with bodily torments
in order to distract her,
and assail her peace of soul,
the soul being in great nakedness of spirit
at this time.
The soul's protection is withdrawal
into deep recollection in God.

3–5.   The Holy Spirit's action in us has brought us to a very high state of union with God (this corresponds to the Sixth Mansion in *The Interior Castle*). St. Teresa herself remained ten years in this state of spiritual betrothal. But this union is not, as yet, uninterrupted; rather it is intermittent, felt and experienced at intervals. The "vineyard is now in flower": there has been remarkable increase in the virtues, which now seem easy, requiring little effort; the Bridegroom is acting in us.

Despite this, there is still awareness of imperfection. We are still subject to temptation, the imagination is difficult to control, and our lower nature asserts itself—"the flesh lusteth against the spirit." Like foxes, thought to be asleep, and no longer a danger, they have been lying in wait for the opportunity to attack. Here is a lurking enemy which must be sought out, "caught," and destroyed if the vineyard is to put forth its fruit.

It is implied here that it is possible to conquer these sensory movements and desires, but not by one's own strength. It is not in the soul's power to be free of them. We call on the intercession of the angels, whose special duty it is to assist us against the demons, who make use of the imagination and sense appetites to prevent our progress in love and virtue.

6.   St. John instructs us on how to proceed when the devil is so active, stimulating the appetites and imagination (he has no power over the intellect and will), and even attacking with bodily torments. His advice is "to enter into recollection very quickly, returning within ourselves. The devil knows that once we have entered into this recollection, he is unable to do us any harm." To "disturb the soul's peace"—that is always his aim.

7.   Cf. Cant. 6:11: "My soul troubles me
        because of the chariots of Aminadab."
        Cf. Cant. 2:15: "Catch us the little foxes."

8.   *"while we make a pine-like cluster of roses"*:
        "We" because she,
        in company with the Bridegroom,
        fashions a bouquet
        of the flowers of virtues
        which seem to be His
        as well as hers.

9.   Like a pine cone,
        one perfect whole of strong virtues.

10.   *"let no one appear on the hill"*:
        To attain this Divine union
        the soul needs solitude—
        withdrawal from all natural knowledge and affection,
        sensory and rational—
        in the memory, intellect, will,
        the imagination, and the senses.

11.   Only when the faculties
        cease working and become idle,
        empty of their natural operations,
        can the soul attend to God with love.

7–11. We find ourselves at this stage hard put to reconcile apparent contradictions in the commentary. We have read, for example, of "habitual peace in the visits of the Beloved" (Introduction, Stanza 16); "the soul's virtues . . . a sweet-tasting wine"; and now, "the soul [is] in great nakedness of spirit at this time." The fact is that despite deep-down peace of mind, there is a good deal of disturbance outwardly. Not that joy and sorrow alternate; the two apparently contradictory elements are present simultaneously, and on the exterior there seems to be anything but peace.

The devil does not give up easily, and he has power to afflict the body, and indirectly the soul, by causing nameless fears arising from distressing phantasms or imaginations in the mind, arousing desires and appetites long since thought to be under control. In short, this is a time of severe temptation, which causes great distress, as we cannot know whether or not we have given in to the evil suggestions.

Not that the temptations are necessarily centered on impurity; the devil is cunning and knows that we readily recognize his presence in this kind of temptation. He tempts us rather to pride, or presumption, lack of trust in God, anything that will destroy that peace of mind which comes with the certainty of God's love. The devil's aim is to cause anxiety about our spiritual state. To recognize the temptation is the first step toward combating it, and the way to deal with it is not to try to fight temptation, as before, but to withdraw into a deeper recollection of spirit, in God. We feel the need for solitude.

This is the progessive "entering within" of which St. Teresa speaks in *The Interior Castle*—entering into the center of the soul where God dwells, where the devil is powerless to enter. At the same time, we practice the ordinary virtues with more determination, not now alone, but with the Bridegroom. Conscious of the "joint effort" which now makes virtue seem easy, we can say, with St. Paul, "with Christ I am nailed to the Cross . . . when I am weak, then I am strong."

Introduction

1.   The absence of the Beloved
      causes great suffering.
      Any communication or converse with creatures
      increases the torment.
      Fearing anything which prevents her coming
      into the presence of the Beloved,
      she speaks:

      "Be still, deadening north wind;
      come, south wind. You that waken love,
      breathe through my garden;
      let its scented fragrance flow,
      and the beloved will feed amid the flowers."

2.   Besides this, she suffers spiritual dryness,
      so she does two things:
      she practices continual prayer,
      and she invokes the Holy Spirit.
      He it is who, moving her to exercise the virtues,
      leads her to rejoice in the Bridegroom.

3.   *"Be still, deadening north wind"*:
      The north wind is cold,
      drying and withering flowers and plants.
      Here it means spiritual dryness.

Commentary

      "Be still, deadening north wind":
      The spiritual dryness and absence of the Beloved
      have the deadening effect of the north wind,
      extinguishing the satisfaction
      and delights of the virtues.
      Therefore, the soul invokes the Holy Spirit,
      the refreshing "south wind."

4.   *"come, south wind. You that waken love"*:
      She is wholly enkindled and refreshed,
      awakening the will and the appetite
      to love of God.

Theme: Spiritual dryness gives way to the peace of the Holy Spirit, communicating the Bridegroom.

1–3.   The Beloved is absent and we find no satisfaction arising from the virtues which God has given. The result is spiritual dryness, leaving us desolate, as the north wind leaves a parched land, dry and arid. But there is a remedy: the Holy Spirit, the Divine "breath" of God; like the gentle, refreshing south wind, bringing refreshing rain and coolness. He answers our prayer for relief.

4.   The result of the gentle infusion of the Spirit is refreshment, light, peace; we are enkindled in God's love.

5.   *"breathe through my garden"*:
        The garden of the soul.
        The flowers of perfection and virtues
        come to life and begin to grow.
        Note: not breathing *in* the soul,
        but through it.
        To breathe through is to touch and put in motion
        these virtues and perfections already given.
        The soul does not always experience and enjoy
        the acquired or infused virtues;
        they remain within her
        like flowers enclosed in a bud,
        or aromatic spices whose scent is not perceived
        until shaken and uncovered.

6.   God sometimes thus reveals
        the beauty of the soul
        in all its perfection and beauty.

7.   *"let its scented fragrance flow"*:
        The experience is not only within the soul,
        but is manifest to others.
        It begets an inner, mysterious dignity
        and greatness in the soul
        which cause awe and respect in others,
        aware as they are
        of the soul's closeness
        and familiarity with God.
        Compare Moses and St. Paul
        (Ex. 34:29–30; 2 Cor. 3:7).

5.   Just as the flowers come to life with the rain-bearing wind,
        so do the virtues now show themselves; already present, they
        are now put in motion and perfected by the influence of the
        Holy Spirit. Not that we are always conscious of the virtues,
        or enjoy their effects. This figure of speech—of the "flowering"
        of the virtues—reminds us of the theology of the gifts of the
        Holy Spirit: the virtues are infused at baptism but only with
        difficulty "go into action," until the gifts of the Holy Spirit activate
        them, making their practice easy and pleasant. The wheels of
        a cart may grind along with difficulty until the axle is greased;
        an oarsman may have difficulty making progress until a good
        wind catches the sail. Then all is pleasant, swift, and easy;
        similarly, the gifts of the Holy Spirit, breathing "through" the
        soul, make virtue seem easy. What was before hidden, now
        becomes evident.

        Perhaps we do not call on the Holy Spirit as we should.
        Especially in times of difficulty in prayer, it is He who "comes
        to the aid of our weakness, telling us what to pray for and
        how to pray for it" (cf. Romans 8:26, 27).

6–7.   "Sometimes," but not always, God reveals both to ourselves
        and to others the working of His grace. Without detriment to
        humility we can say, with the Blessed Virgin, "How wonderful
        I am, because of the wonderful things He has done in me."
        And surely we will think of Our Lady when reading paragraph 7.
        Her joy and serenity of spirit in every situation, whether in joy
        or in sorrow, must have been obvious to those about her—
        the "inner, mysterious dignity and greatness in the soul which
        cause awe and respect in others". Now God allows something
        of Himself to be seen in us, so that others realize our "closeness
        and familiarity" with Him.

        Not, indeed, all others. In the case of St. Thérèse of Lisieux
        some of her sisters felt this about her, some did not, as the
        canonisation process shows. Some people were disappointed
        with St. Teresa because she did not fit into their idea of
        "saintliness"; some of those who associated with St. John of
        the Cross failed to recognize his sanctity. God allows this, and
        the fault can be in the other person. Note the example of the
        Pharisees and Our Lord.

8.   In this breathing of the Holy Spirit in the soul,
        the Bridegroom, the Son of God,
        is sublimely communicated.
        He sends His Spirit to prepare His dwelling,
        adorning the garden of her soul
        in preparation for His coming.
        She gains the perfect exercise of the virtues,
        with the continuation of delight and sweetness
        in the exercise of these virtues.
        Compare Cant. 1:11: the "flowering spikenard"
        is the soul,
        giving off the fragrance of her virtues
        for the enjoyment of her Beloved,
        dwelling in her.

9.   Hence, the importance of greatly desiring
        the divine breeze of the Holy Spirit,
        and of asking for it;
        it brings much glory and good to the soul.
        Compare Cant. 4:16: "Come, South Wind,
        and blow through my garden."
        The bride knows that the Bridegroom delights in this preparation
        for His coming.

10.   "and the Beloved will feed amid the flowers":
        Amid the flowers
        of the soul's virtues, gifts, and perfections,
        communicated to her by the Bridegroom.
        He takes His delight in the soul,
        prepared by the Holy Spirit,
        dwelling there with great pleasure.
        Compare Proverbs 8:31: "My delights are to be
        with the children of men."
        Compare also Cant. 6:1, 2:
        "My Beloved pastures in the gardens,
        He feeds among the lilies."

8. Everything is the work of the Holy Spirit; this is His precise function, His special work—to prepare us for the coming of the Bridegroom. He has no other work than to bring us to Christ, who in turn brings us the Father. Through Him "the Bridegroom, the Son of God, is sublimely communicated." This is especially so of the Holy Spirit's action in the Eucharist: the outpouring of the Spirit from the glorious Risen Christ in turn brings us back to Him, deepening our integration into Him, our union with and assimilation to Him—a truth too seldom associated with Eucharistic action.

9. Both *The Spiritual Canticle* and *The Living Flame* of St. John of the Cross might well be called treatises on the Holy Spirit. Here the Saint is emphatic: we must both desire and ask for the Holy Spirit. The implication is that if we do, He will bring much glory and good to the soul.

    Reading St. John of the Cross one senses a certain urgency in impressing on his readers the importance of the Holy Spirit. There is no emphasis whatever in his writings on any particular "devotion." He warns against extravagance and excesses in this matter; but there is constant reference throughout to the need for invoking of the Holy Spirit. There is no substitute for this devotion.

10. The delight which the Beloved, Christ, takes in us at this time is due to the fact that the Holy Spirit has prepared the dwelling place for Him in communicating the "flowers" of virtues; finding this, the Bridegroom communicates himself, with His own virtues and perfections, so that there is a mutual sharing and exchange, as is becoming in bride and Bridegroom. "His delight is to be with the children of men"—this is the mystery of God's condescension.

    What is marriage if not a mutual giving of oneself to the other, "perpetually and exclusively"? We have seen that this communication of the virtues and perfections of the Risen Christ is the first fruit of the Eucharist.

Introduction

1.   The soul often experiences intense suffering
at this time,
aware as she is, on the one hand,
of the surpassing riches she possesses
and, on the other,
of the obstacles within herself
to the enjoyment of them.
Her presence in the body, the appetites,
and inordinate movements of the flesh
make her feel like a noble, wealthy Lord
who is imprisoned, subject to a thousand miseries,
his dominion confiscated,
he himself even refused a little food.

2.   So, in the hope
that these sensual desires and appetites will be subdued,
she speaks:

"You nymphs of Judea,
while among flowers and roses
the amber spreads its perfume,
stay away, there on the outskirts::
desire not to touch our thresholds."

Theme: May the higher, spiritual nature dominate the unruly sensual appetites and desires.

1.   It is characteristic of this stage of the spiritual journey that both joy and the suffering are intensified. Despite all that has gone before, we never escape from the bondage of the flesh with its inordinate movements and temptations. So far from being discouraged at this, we find comfort in the assurance of the Saint given in this stanza. We are not duly perturbed by what St. Paul calls our "lower nature."

Like him, we ask to be "delivered from the body of his death," but no matter to what heights God may raise us, we must never be surprised that temptations of this kind may come; in fact they can be most distressing at this time because of one's nearness to God, and the heightened awareness of God's goodness and holiness. We can be "subject to a thousand miseries," despite the "surpassing richness" of God's gifts.

St. Teresa devotes a whole chapter of *The Interior Castle* (Mans. VI.1) to describing the great trials experienced—"so terrible as to be intolerable."

2.   The experience can be distressing to the point of being terrifying: "compared only to the sufferings of hell" (I.C. Mans. VI.1). St. Thérèse of Lisieux experienced terrible darkness and temptation in the last eighteen months of her life, seemingly without respite.

It is interesting to note that Stanzas 18 and 19 correspond to Stanzas 31 and 32 in the First Redaction of *The Spiritual Canticle* (see "Introduction").

Commentary

3. The bride asks that the lower, sensory part
be stilled,
with its disturbances in the flesh,
and not disquiet the higher, spiritual part of the soul.

4. As girls try to attract lovers to themselves
by their gifts and graces,
so the lower sensory part
tries to dominate the intellect and will.
"Judea," because weak and carnal,
blind, like the Judean people.

5. "*while among flowers and roses*":
The virtues and faculties of the soul—
memory, intellect, and will.

6. "*the amber spreads its perfume*":
Amber, the Bridegroom's divine spirit,
abiding in her, overflowing,
communicating itself in the faculties
and virtues in the soul.

7. "*stay away, there on the outskirts*":
That is, the interior sense faculties—
sensible memory, phantasy, imagination—
and the exterior sense faculties—
hearing, sight, smell.
These the soul asks to remain quiet,
not to distract the rational, spiritual parts of the soul
from its peace and communion with God.
It is to be remembered
that what is felt in the lower part of the senses
is naturally communicated
to the inner, rational part.

8. "*desire not to touch our thresholds*":
Do not even touch,
by first movements,
the higher part;
leave the soul
in the quietude and peace
she enjoys.

3–4.   The metaphor seems strained; the lower part of our nature, the flesh and its allurements, is likened to sensual young girls who, weak and carnal in their desires, try to entice others into sin. So our lower nature tries to tempt and to dominate the higher, spiritual part. This conflict never ceases; unless God directly intervenes, we are prone to sensual desire and temptation as long as we remain in this mortal life, and we should not be surprised or discouraged at this.

5–6.   Again, the Holy Spirit, spreading His perfume like amber in the soul, always abiding there despite temptation, continues to communicate His strength and comfort, enlightening the intellect as to the true state of the soul, strengthening the will so that it rises above temptation to sin.

7.   What happens in the "outskirts" of the city, that is, in the senses and imagination, cannot but affect the inner part of the city, or soul, where God dwells. But this is not necessarily so: the presence of the Holy Spirit renders possible the complete domination of intellect and will over the exterior sense faculties. We ask for this, not so much out of fear, at this stage, of yielding to sensual desire as to ensure that we remain at peace, uninterrupted in our communion with God. It is this—loss of our peace of soul—that the devil desires above all.

8.   So, with God's help, we can arrive at the point where even the first movements of temptation are immediately suppressed— that is, theologically speaking, the "first movement," which has no moral significance, because the will is not touched. The "second movement" implies acceptance in the will. Again we see the Saint's insistence on keeping peace of mind. Cf. 1 Peter 3 for the importance of cultivating peace of mind and heart. It is the seed-bed of holiness.

Introduction

1.   The soul suffers
      from the awareness of the body's inability
      to support the spiritual communications
      and delights of God.
      She asks God to confer His favors
      outside the body.
      Compare Wisdom 9:15: "The body . . . is a burden to the soul."
      2 Cor. 12:2, 2 Cor. 4:

      "Hide yourself my love;
      turn your face to gaze upon the mountains,
      think not to speak;
      but look at those companions
      going with her through strange islands."

2.   The bride asks the Bridegroom for four things (see 3, 4, 5, 6).

3.   *"Hide yourself, my love"*:
      Manifest yourself in secret,
      hidden from mortal eye.

Theme: May the spiritual communications of the Beloved be communicated to the Spirit alone, not to the senses.

Introduction:

1–3.   We are still in the stage of spiritual espousal, which, despite the fact that it is a very high state, is still one of purification. The body is not yet able to sustain the purely spiritual communications of God; it gradually adapts itself, but it is a painful process, a kind of protestation of the body against the invasion of the Divine.

St. John speaks elsewhere of the gradual "spiritualization" which takes place as the inflowing of God intensifies. Here Chapters 5–10 of Book II of *The Dark Night* should be read: "When the divine light of contemplation strikes a soul not entirely illumined, it causes spiritual darkness . . ." St. Paul speaks of not knowing whether the sublime vision he had of the third heaven was received "in the body, or out of it." St. John concludes that it must have been outside the body, so sublime were the secret words that he heard; the body would have been an obstacle to this.

Both St. John and St. Teresa agree that it is this weakness of the body which results in such things as flights of the spirit, ecstasies, and raptures, which, though from God, occur because of the body's weakness and its inability to cope with the supernatural. It is significant that in the last stage of Spiritual Marriage, these extraordinary occurrences cease almost entirely.

4.   *"turn your face to gaze upon the mountains"*:
Let your divinity ["face"] shine
in my intellect
with Divine knowledge;
in my will,
imparting to it Divine love;
in my memory,
with the Divine possession of glory.
"Mountains": memory, intellect, will.
She asks no less
than the essential vision of God.

5.   *"think not to speak"*:
Do not communicate, as before, to the senses,
but let your communications
be so sublime, interior,
that the senses have no part in them.
Cf. 2 Cor. 12:4: "Secrets of which
it is unlawful for men to speak."

6.   *"but look at those companions"*:
Look at the many gifts, virtues, perfections,
you have placed within me
as the token of espousal.

7.   *"going with her through strange islands"*:
Through this strange and wonderful knowledge
which is foreign to the senses,
wholly interior and sublime.

4.   The demand is for nothing less than God himself, His "face"; for the communication of divinity, in itself, not only in signs and manifestations. A bold, excessive desire? It would seem so, but now we know that this is the very desire of God himself, to give himself totally, as He is in himself. We ask for "Divine knowledge," to know God as He knows himself; for "Divine love," loving with God's love; and for "Divine possession of glory." We recall the Last Supper: "Eternal life is knowing Thee, Father" (John 14:7)—that is, with that knowing which is a taking possession of in love, knowing God with His own knowledge "so that the love you have bestowed on me may dwell in them," "that they may be where I am, so as to see my glory," referring to this life, not only to the next.

This spiritual espousal and Spiritual Marriage are an anticipation, a bringing forward, of the essential vision of God. And it is this we are now emboldened to ask for: Divine intimacy, God Himself, here and now. The contemplative soul cannot wait; it is divinely impatient. Cf. also John 17:22: "The glory which you have given to me, give to them." 2 Cor. 3:18: "We catch the glory of the Lord as in a mirror . . . borrowing glory from that glory as the Spirit of the Lord enables us."

5–7.   The senses are an obstacle to this Divine sharing of knowledge, love and glory. There is an important implication here: if the senses have no part in these communications, these will be, in the ordinary way of knowledge, unfelt; they will bring no satisfaction to eye, ear, taste, touch, feeling. St. Thérèse of Lisieux, experiencing God in the darkness of faith alone, spike of "unfelt love." It is precisely this that we ask for here and now.

Introduction

1.   The attainment of Spiritual Marriage,
which the soul hopes for,
requires not only the purification
of the imperfections of the sensory part,
but an unusual strength and fortitude
to bear the sublime embrace of God.
God gives her an amazing strength,
and great purity and beauty.

2.   The Holy Spirit intervenes,
speaking to the Father and the Son
as in the Canticle 8:8–9:
"What shall we do for our sister
on the day of her courtship?"
Let us build silver bulwarks and defences,
heroic, strong virtues
clothed with faith (silver).
These are the foundation (wall)
of the Spiritual Marriage,
and the Bridegroom
rests in the strength of these virtues.
The bride must hold
the "door" of her will open
in order to pronounce her "Yes"—
her consent, true and complete,
to the betrothal preceding Spiritual Marriage.

3.   The soul answers, "I am a wall
and my breasts are as a tower":
my soul is strong and my love deep.
Seeing her disposition the Bridegroom replies,
speaking against the oppositions and rebellions
from the senses and the devil:

Theme: The natural appetites and passions are brought under control; peace results.

1. From beginning to end, the work is God's, through the intervention of the Holy Spirit. It is He who carries out the work of purification which is necessary, and without His help we would be unable to support His presence, His "sublime embrace."

2. The particular grace given to the Apostles at Pentecost was that of fortitude—grace and strength to face persecution and opposition where previously they had lacked the courage to proclaim the Kingdom. Fortitude is needed here; it is the particular gift of the Holy Spirit. In order to give ourselves entirely to God, to pronounce our "Yes" to His loving advance, great courage is necessary, and if many fail in the spiritual life, it is often because they are afraid of the "leap in the dark" which the complete surrender to God in faith implies and demands.

    Many of us fail to turn to the Holy Spirit; we rely too much on ourselves; we falter; we are afraid to love, afraid of love. The "Yes" is that of espousal, not that of the final surrender of Spiritual Marriage. The foundation is being surely laid; the Holy Spirit is imparting the strength for the heroic, strong virtues which, practiced in faith, attract the Bridegroom and are the foundation of the Spiritual Marriage. In these He will rest.

3. Now it is the Bridegroom who speaks, in reply to the bride's assurance; she is strong with the strength of the Holy Spirit, and the same spirit has implanted in her a deep love. Cf. St. Paul: "The spirit of love has been poured forth in our hearts." Seeing dispositions, finding the spirit there, the Bridegroom commands the rebellious movements of the senses and appetites to cease.

"Swift-winged birds,
lions, stags, and leaping roes,
mountains, lowlands, and river banks,
waters, winds, and heat of the day
watching terrors of the night:

By the pleasant lyres
and the siren's song, I conjure you,
cease your anger
and touch not the wall,
that the bride may sleep secure."

Commentary

4.   The Bridegroom answers the bride's request.
He subjects
the sensory appetites and desires
to the control of the higher faculties,
commanding also
the useless wanderings of the imagination to cease once and
for all.
he brings the irascible and concupiscible powers
under the control
of the memory, intellect, and will,
as far as it is possible in this life.
He commands the four passions—
joy, hope, fear, sorrow—
to submit to the control of reason.
All this results
from the surrender and spiritual communication
made by the Bridegroom,
with its accompanying delight,
sweetness, and strength imparted to the soul.
God vitally and transforms the soul
into Himself.

4.   The lower, sense appetites and desires now, at the command of the Bridegroom, are subjected to control of the higher faculties; intellect and will are now in command, once and for all.

A tremendous grace, indeed; one of the effects of original sin is nullified; the lower nature becomes subject to the higher; reason and will are in complete command. Through this intimate relationship we are gradually becoming ourselves; gradually reaching true "fulfillment," true maturity. It is the gradual, vital transformation of the soul into God.

5.   *'swift-winged birds'*:
        The restless wanderings
        of the imagination,
        which displease the soul.
        By the "pleasant lyres":
        by the sweetness and delight
        experienced in this high state.

6.   "*lions, stags, and leaping roes*":
        The concupiscible and irascible powers,
        causing either undue cowardice
        or daring in the soul.

7.   The Bridegroom intervenes
        to control anger and concupiscence;
        not that they cease,
        but what is inordinate
        is controlled.

8.   "*mountains, lowlands, and river banks*":
        The vicious and inordinate acts
        of the memory, intellect, and will;
        extreme either from excess or defect.
        The "lyres," or the sweetness
        God bestows on the soul,
        perfect the faculties of the soul;
        it is so carried out of itself
        that everything immoderate ceases.

5.   St. Teresa frequently refers to the difficulty of controlling the imagination. It is as difficult to control as "wild horses"; "as well try to stop the movement of the heavens." Many good people cease to pray because of a wandering imagination, which they find impossible to control; they complain of continual distraction. They should not be discouraged. Prayer is in the will, not the imagination, and no amount of indeliberate distraction can spoil our prayer (cf. I.C. Mans. IV.1).

Here God intervenes. Just as the virtues became easier, now, with His help, there is no difficulty in controlling the imagination. It does not wander, and remains subject to the will and to our desire to center our whole heart and mind on God. In the earlier stages of contemplative prayer, it was possible for the will to be centered entirely on God, yet the imagination remained free, restlessly flitting from one subject to another, causing distress. Cf. chapter XXXI, paragraph 6, of *The Way of Perfection*. (Note that St. Teresa sometimes uses "understanding" for "imagination").

6–7.   The passions, or movements of the sense appetite—either love, desire, joy, hatred, aversion, sadness (these are called "concupiscible") or hope, daring, despair, fear, anger ("irascible")— are brought under control.

8.   The two extremes, "mountains" and "lowlands," represent what is vicious or inordinate, extreme through excess or defect; that which is seriously sinful. The "river banks" represent that which is neither high nor low, but imperfect. The Bridegroom indicates that henceforth everything that is immoderate will cease. Note that "mountains" was given an entirely different meaning in Stanza 19—namely the faculties of the soul.

9.   *"Waters, winds, and heat of the day*
        watching terrors of the night":
        The four passions:
        sorrow, hope, joy, and fear.
        Cf. Ps. 68:2: "Save me, my God,
        for the waters have come even to my soul"—
        that is, sorrow ("waters");
        the emotions of hope ("winds")
        flying toward the absent object
        (cf. Ps. 118:131);
        the joy which inflames the heart
        like fire ("heat of the day").
        Cf. Ps. 38:4: "My heart grew hot within me
        and in my meditation
        a fire shall be kindled."
        The fears experienced in this state
        ("terrors of the night")
        are caused by God;
        but sometimes they are caused by the devil,
        resulting in distraction,
        conflict, sorrow, dread in the senses,
        in order to disturb the peace of the soul;
        hence, "terrors of the night,"
        These are not natural fears,
        but spiritual fears.

10.   The Bridegroom commands the four passions
        to cease and be calm,
        giving the soul
        riches, strength, and satisfaction
        it did not previously experience
        in the practice of the virtues.
        While, for instance,
        she exercises sorrow and compassion,
        the feelings formerly accompanying these
        have ceased;
        the strength and perfection of the virtues
        are increased.
        We think here of the virtues
        of the Virgin Mother and St. Paul.
        God did not exempt them from feeling
        and suffering from events,
        but their state of suffering
        did not consist in the feeling of sorrow.

9. Confusion may arise regarding the understanding of the passions: the passion of hope, for instance, must not be confused with the theological virtue of hope. The passions, or emotions, are neither good nor bad in themselves; they are the natural movements of our sense desires in the presence of persons, places, things which naturally excite feelings of joy, sorrow, hope, or fear. When governed according to right reason, aided by the grace of God, they become the nurseries of the virtues. When they are in command, dominating the reason, they produce habits of vice. The devil can bring about conflict in us by causing undue fear, anxiety, or depression. Sometimes God allows these fears, which are spiritual in nature. These fears, St. John says, are characteristic of spiritual people. "Fears" are not to be confused with "scruples"!

10. The time has come for these passions to cease troubling us; something unusual, seemingly contradictory, takes place. While practicing and exercising, for example, sorrow and compassion, we find that we rise above the ordinary feelings which we would otherwise experience; there is no disturbance of spirit, peace of soul remains, yet there is genuine sorrow and compassion. The strength and the perfection of the virtues are increased, but they are now exercised in peace, tranquillity, and serenity of spirit.

This is a gift of God; we think of the petitions of the Mass after the "Pater Noster", in each of which we ask for delivery from anxiety, conflict, disturbance of mind—in a word, for peace. St. John likens this state to that of the angels, who exercise compassion, mercy, and love without the feeling accompanying these virtues. However, as in the case of the Blessed Virgin, God may allow us to feel and to suffer.

11.   The desires of the passion of hope
      no longer affect her;
      being now satisfied
      with union with God in this life
      she has nothing to hope for from the world,
      nor anything to desire spiritually.
      In life and death
      she is conformed to the will of God.
      Her constant prayer is
      "Thy will be done."
      Her desire for the vision of God
      is painless.
      The emotions of joy no longer influence her;
      what she now enjoys
      is the fountain of these waters
      "leaping up to life everlasting."
      She has now no concern
      about having or not having
      more or less than before.

12.   Not that accidental joys
      are no longer experienced;
      they simply do not add anything to her joy;
      she turns immediately within herself
      to the great joy of her new life with God.
      We could compare this kind of joy
      to that of God,
      whose essential joy in Himself
      cannot be changed or added to,
      being eminently above all accidental joys.

13.   While on the one hand
      the soul is capable
      of receiving new spiritual joys,
      they seem as nothing to her;
      everything seems as something new,
      yet as already received.

14.   The excellence of the illumination
      which the bride receives from the Bridegroom
      at this time
      is so wonderful as to be beyond description.

11.   No longer is there hope or joy in worldly things; we have all
       we can hope for in God; no worldly joy distracts from the
       enjoyment of God. We simply are not concerned about having,
       or not having, what before we considered necessary. Job knew
       this kind of detachment: "The Lord gave, the Lord has taken
       away, blessed be the name of the Lord."

12.   St. John immediately corrects any wrong impression: it is not
       that we begin to live in some kind of dream world, taking no
       interest in the people and things around us; it is rather that
       the joys and sorrows of life simply do not affect us as before.
       There is one great joy in life—God. Having found Him, nothing
       else really matters; everything that happens is seen and judged
       in a new light; God is always the point of reference in every
       new situation. "Let nothing disturb you" is not an ideal but
       a way of life. St. John suggests that this is the kind of joy
       experienced by God, an essential joy which cannot be disturbed
       by events and which cannot be changed or added to.

13.   Even spiritual joys are accepted in this way; they are recognized,
       and accepted gratefully, but there is no undue excitement.
       St. Thérèse of Lisieux received a grace which can be described
       as a transverberation of the heart; she told no one about it
       till she was on her deathbed, and then seemed to attribute
       no great importance to it. This is the ultimate in detachment.

14.   All this comes from God alone; it is "wonderful beyond
       description" and a characteristic mark of high sanctity.

15.   No fears or darkness
        can now touch the soul;
        the devil can no longer frighten
        or molest her.
        In God she enjoys all delight,
        all sweetness and abiding peace.
        "The peaceful and tranquil soul
        is like a continual banquet" (Pr. 15:15).
        She has achieved the peace of God
        which surpasses all understanding (Phil. 4:7).

16.   *"By the pleasant lyres*
        And the siren's song, I conjure you":
        This describes the habitual delight and peace,
        the "siren's song" which enraptures,
        making us forget all else.

17.   *"cease your anger"*:
        The troubles and disturbances
        causing disquiet.

18.   *"touch not the wall"*:
        The enclosure of peace,
        and the "wall" of virtues and perfections
        protecting the soul.
        Compare Cant. 4:12: "My sister
        is an enclosed garden."

19.   *"that the bride may sleep secure"*:
        No door is now closed to the soul;
        she can enjoy this gentle sleep of love
        at will.
        Compare Cant. 3:5: "Do not stir
        or wake the beloved until she wishes."

15.   A delightful state indeed; we are beyond the fears and the
       darkness which formerly oppressed us; at last the devil is
       powerless to frighten or harm us. It is a state of enduring peace.
       St. Peter speaks of "the imperishable jewel of a gentle and
       quiet spirit, which in God's eyes is very precious" (1 Peter
       3). This is the "peace which surpasses understanding" of Phil.
       4:7. Christ's last bequest to us was "My peace I give you, my
       peace I leave with you." She enjoys all peace, tastes all
       sweetness, delights in every delight. St. John adds that this joy
       and peace are "indescribable."

16–19. The "pleasant lyres and the siren's song": the habitual, uninter-
       rupted joy of this state end all disquiet ("anger") and
       disturbance. The enclosure of abiding peace cannot now be
       broken; we are like the bride of the Canticle, "an enclosed
       garden" where all is restful, tranquil, beyond reach of turmoil.

       This deep, abiding peace is habitual in the sense that we can
       experience it at will. We are now perfectly prepared for the
       Bridegroom's final advances; spiritual espousal is about to be
       sealed with the marriage bond.

DIVISION III
PERFECT UNION

Introduction

1.   Like the good shepherd rejoicing
      at having found the lost sheep,
      and the woman the lost drachma,
      the Bridegroom rejoices
      at the soul's liberation
      from sensuality and the devil.
      He calls on the angels and saints also
      to rejoice with him;
      Compare Canticle 4:11.
      His bride is now the joy of His heart;
      He takes her in His arms
      and goes forth with her
      from the bridal chamber (Ps. 18:6).

      "The bride has entered
      the sweet garden so much desired,
      and she rests to her delight,
      reclining her neck
      on the gentle arms of her beloved."

Theme: Liberation; beginning of total transformation in the Beloved; loving intimacy.

1. St. Teresa says of this "entering the sweet garden of delight," which is the Seventh Mansion, that Our Lord "needs an abiding place in the soul, as He has in Heaven" (I.C. Mans. VII.1). It becomes a "second Heaven." Indeed it is a foretaste of heaven. The bride, liberated "from sensuality and the devil," is now the joy of the Bridegroom's heart; with all the realism of the Song of Songs, St. John of the Cross, more poetically and perhaps more realistically than St. Teresa, says, "He takes her in His arms and goes forth with her from the bridal chamber."

    Our two Saints, who experienced this wonderful intimacy with God, in searching for a metaphor to convey the incomparable closeness of this union, invariably fell back on the comparison of marriage. That, after all, is what the sacred writer, inspired by God, did in writing the Song of Songs. The metaphor denotes a reality which is otherwise indescribable, just as every figure of speech used in the Scriptures to describe man's union with God must remain a figure of speech only. "Mystical body," "vine and branches," the bridal image, even fatherhood and sonship, point to a reality (union in love of God with man) but they always fall far short of that reality.

    The same is true, then, of the term "Spiritual Marriage." St. Paul, in chapter 5 of the Ephesians, teaches that marriage is a sacramental expression of God's union (or marriage) with man in the life of grace bestowed at baptism, which is deepened and intensified throughout his life. It is not that we think of earthly marriage, and reason then to the union of God with man; it is the other way about (Eph. 5:21–33). Similarly, in thinking of the Spiritual Marriage, we contemplate first the wonder of God's union of love with man, and from that we reason to the notion of marriage in its truest and noblest sense: a union of minds, heart, and spirit achieved through the flesh, according to God's design; but "the incitement of the flesh gives way to that which transcends it" (Jean Guitton). Compare the marriage of Mary and Joseph; the reality of marriage was achieved from the beginning.

Commentary

2.   Now the bride has sought
       to remove all obstacles
       to full union of Spiritual Marriage
       and invoked the Holy Spirit.
       First the Bridegroom tells
       how she has reached this state
       of Spiritual Marriage
       which He desired as much as the bride.
       Second, He tells
       of the properties of this state,
       resting in delight,
       laying her neck
       on the gentle arms of the Beloved.

3.   Now begins the Spiritual Marriage,
       which is incomparably greater
       than the spiritual espousal,
       being a total transformation in the Beloved,
       in which each surrenders
       the entire possession of self
       with consummation in loving union.
       The soul thereby becomes Divine;
       becoming God through participation,
       insofar as this is possible in this life.
       I think this never happens
       without the soul being confirmed in grace,
       the highest state attainable in this life.
       Just as in marriage
       there are two in one flesh,
       in this consummation
       of the Spiritual Marriage of God and the soul,
       there are two natures
       in one spirit and love.
       "He who is joined to the Lord
       is one spirit with Him" (1 Cor. 6:17).
       This union resembles the union
       of the light of a star or candle
       with the light of the sun,
       for what really sheds light
       is not the star or candle,
       but the sun.

2–3. The "total transformation in the Beloved" has begun; St. Teresa says that the difference between the spiritual espousal and Spiritual Marriage is that betrothed persons are still free to break off the engagement, whereas in marriage "they cannot be separated anymore." "Of course," she says, "it has nothing to do with the body; this union takes place in the deepest center of the soul." St. John reminds us that "each surrenders the entire possession of self" to the other.

The condescension of God! He surrenders Himself to us! There is food for prayerful meditation here; perhaps we would never accept this as possible if we had not the testimony of our Saints, who record what they and others have really experienced. The assurance of the mystics adds a further dimension to God's revelation of Himself in Scripture and tradition. In the writings of those Saints and holy people whose writings are approved by the Church we have a treasury of knowledge about God; we do not order our lives according to these revelations, but when used wisely and with discretion they help us in understanding the infinite love and tenderness of God.

"The soul . . . becomes Divine." This is no figure of speech. Yet it must be understood in St. John's terms. The soul becomes Divine "by participation." God alone is Divine by nature; Christ, the Word made Flesh, is Divine by nature. We never become Divine by nature but by participation in the Divine nature.

Raised to the heights of Spiritual Marriage, we still remain ourselves, still remain human in the fullest sense; indeed, now we are truly human, truly persons, truly mature, for only in God is true maturity to be found. The goal of all our spiritual striving has been attained. The planet has not light of its own, but it shines with a real light, the light of the sun. Our Blessed Lady understood this, and in reading this section of *The Spiritual Canticle* we should keep her always in mind. We are sons of God, not in the same way as Christ, who alone is Son of God by nature. We are sons of God by grace, by which we participate in, and become sharers in, the natural sonship of Christ, "the first-born of many brothers." God makes us "sharers in the divine nature, calling us to His own glory and excellence" (2 Peter 1:3).

4.   *"the sweet garden so much desired"*:
God is the "sweet garden".
God calls the soul,
after betrothal,
placing her in His flowering garden
to consummate
this most joyful state of marriage with Him.
The union wrought between the two natures
and the communication
of the Divine to the human is such
that even though neither changes its being,
both appear to be God.
Yet in this life
the union cannot be perfect.

5.   Compare Cant. 5:1: "Come and enter my garden,
my sister, my bride,
for now I have gathered my myrrh
with my fragrant spices."
Sister and bride, in the love
with which she surrendered to Him
before the marriage.
The garden is the Bridegroom Himself,
now as never before
communicating himself so intimately
that the bride seems placed in His arms,
in a true embrace
in which she lives the life of God.
Compare Gal. 2:20: "I live, now not I,
but Christ lives in me."
No longer can she feel any distaste,
Just as God is incapable of this;
for the delight of God's glory
is experienced and enjoyed
in the substance of the soul,
now transformed into Him.

4. Once established that the union is entirely spiritual—"two natures in one spirit and love" (paragraph 3)—St. John boldly uses the language of conjugal love: "to consummate this most joyful state of marriage." The Divine is communicated to the human but "neither changes its being." Note that the union is not as perfect as that of heaven; St. Teresa says, "It cannot be fulfilled perfectly in this life" (I.C. Mans. VII.2). "Both appear to be God" is a literal translation of the Spanish "*cada parece Dios*"; more accurately, of course, St. John might have said, "the soul appears to be God."

5. The Saint turns, naturally enough, to the Canticle of Canticles, in which God is referred to as the "garden enclosed"; now the terms "sister", "bride," can be used, as the loving surrender is complete; and because of this, the Bridegroom gives himself totally in return. The new life in God can only be described in terms of a loving embrace: we are in the arms of God, in a loving intimacy in which the Bridegroom communicates Himself as never before.

Perhaps only those who have experienced this overwhelming tenderness and condescension of God can read St. Paul's words—"I have no life of my own anymore; Christ lives in me; Christ is my life"—without surprise. God is incapable of feeling distaste, displeasure in anything. So it is now with us; there is the delight and joy deep down in the very inner substance of the soul; the soul cannot now be really disturbed; no earthly consideration, no passing anxiety, frustration, or suffering can disturb the peace of soul now experienced. It is a total transformation into Christ, whose words, "My peace I give unto you," now have meaning.

6.   *"and she rests to her delight,*
        reclining her neck":
        With that same strength
        with which she conquered sensuality before,
        now in that same strength ["neck"]
        she can endure
        so intimate an embrace.

7.   *"on the gentle arms of her Beloved"*:
        Her strength and weakness
        are now united to the strength of God;
        the "arms" of God now become her strength
        in which she is sheltered
        and protected against all evils.
        Compare Cant. 8:1: "Who will give you to me
        for my brother
        that I may find you alone outside
        and kiss you, and no one despise me?"
        This means:
        All my passions subdued,
        I found you in solitude
        and nakedness of spirit;
        denuded of all natural and spiritual impurity,
        I kiss you, undisturbed by the flesh,
        the world, the devil, or any appetite.
        So the soul can say,
        "Winter is now past, the rain is gone,
        and the flowers have appeared in our land."

6–7.   There is repeated emphasis of this experience of the intimacy
       of God requiring a special gift of God in order to bear it; the
       human cannot support the divine. Moses veiled his face in
       a symbolic gesture, expressing the inability of man to bear
       God's presence. How much more his loving embrace! The effects
       of God's communication of himself now become evident: not
       only His virtues are communicated, but His strength; the
       Omnipotent so shares His power with a creature that no evil
       can now befall it. Not only sensuality, but what formerly
       appeared as evil, suffering, the cross, the daily vexations and
       frustrations of everyday living, are now seen in the perspective
       of God.

       Trials are borne as Christ bore His Cross; there is suffering
       indeed, but it is seen in a new light, borne with "the strength
       of God, the arms of God." One thing above all mattered to
       Christ in the midst of His sufferings: the Father's will. The inner
       strength to bear the sufferings came from this loving relationship
       with the Father, though humanly speaking He would not have
       chosen this way Himself, as we see in the prayer of the Agony
       in the Garden.

       Cf. Isaias 49:5: "My God is made my strength"; 12:2: "The Lord
       is my strength and my salvation"; Ps. 17: "I will love Thee,
       my Lord, my strength." The solitude and nakedness of spirit
       was the condition of this intimate union. We are now on the
       mountain, where there is "nothing, but the honour and glory
       of God" (cf. the "Sketch of Mt. Carmel" by St. John of the Cross
       in *The Ascent of Mount Carmel*).

Introduction

1. In this high state
    the Bridegroom reveals His wonderful secrets
    to the soul, frequently and readily,
    as to His consort.
    Especially He communicates to her
    the sweet mysteries
    of the Incarnation and Redemption.
    Here He speaks of the Incarnation:

    "Beneath the apple tree
    there you were betrothed to me;
    there I gave you my hand
    and you were raised up again,
    where your mother lost her maidenhood."

Commentary

2. Just as human nature was corrupted
    by means of the forbidden tree
    in the garden of Paradise,
    so on the tree of the Cross,
    it was redeemed and restored
    through His passion and death.

3. *"Beneath the apple tree"*:
    Beneath the apple tree of the Cross,
    not only mankind but each soul
    was espoused to Him.

4,5. *"there you were betrothed . . . maidenhood"*:
    In such a way God shows His wisdom,
    drawing good from evil.
    "your mother": that is, human nature.

Theme: The mystery of the Incarnation is revealed.

1. There are no secrets now between Bridegroom and bride. The greatest mystery of Divine love, the Incarnation and Redemption (we would say, the "Paschal Mystery"), is communicated and revealed "as to a consort"; to one who, by right of marriage must share the deepest secrets of the beloved.

2. The commentary is an explanation, in terms of the Incarnation, of an otherwise difficult passage of the Song of Songs. Christ, the new Adam, redressed the imbalance, healing wounded human nature (St. John uses the strong word "*estragada*," "vitiated," perhaps, rather than "corrupted" (as Luther said)). Not, of course, entirely corrupted; theologians prefer to say "wounded." (The wounded man left for dead, in the Parable of the Good Samaritan, is a simile.)

3. Each one of us, singly and individually, was espoused to Christ on Calvary spiritually—sacramentally really—with the outpouring of the Spirit upon mankind (cf. Jn. 19:30). St. John of the Cross reminds us that it was not only human nature, or mankind in general, that was espoused, but each one of us, personally.

4-5. The Incarnation is the supreme instance of God's power to draw good out of evil.

6.　　　The espousal of the Cross
is not that of which we are speaking.
Each soul receives this espousal at baptism
and it is accomplished immediately.
The espousal of which we speak here
bears reference to perfection
and is achieved only gradually, in stages.
Yet it is all one espousal.
The spiritual espousal
is that of which Ezechiel speaks (Ch. 16:5–14).

6.   Here there seems to be a contradiction. "The espousal of the
Cross is not that of which we are speaking," yet "it is all one
espousal." The mystical experience of espousal which is the
Spiritual Marriage is in fact the perfection and flowering of the
grace of the Holy Spirit which was "poured forth into us" at
baptism. It continues in the life of faith, hope and charity,
intensified by the sacramental life. Obviously not all have this
experience, since not all respond generously to God's love.
Still, as the seed, the seedling, and the tree in full growth can
be described as one, so can baptism and the Spiritual Marriage.
Ezechiel, chapter 16, should be read; this passage made a great
impression on St. Thérèse of Lisieux, intensely aware as she
was of being truly the "Bride of Christ." For her, this was no
mere figure of speech.

Introduction

1.   The bed spoken of
      is the Bridegroom himself,
      the Word, the Son of God,
      upon whom the bride reclines
      in union of love.
      He is the flower of the fields
      and the lily of the valleys
      (Cant. 2:1) Compare Ps. 48:11:
      "The beauty of the field is with me."

      "Our flowery bed,
      bound with dens of lions,
      is hung with purple,
      built up in peace,
      and crowned with a thousand shields of gold."

Commentary

2,3.   *"Our flowery bed"*:
       Compare Cant. 1:15: "Our bed is in flower . . ."
       The Beloved communicates to the soul
       His breast and His love,
       His wisdom, secrets, graces, virtues, gifts,
       so that she seems to rest upon a bed
       made of a variety of sweet, Divine flowers,
       delightful to the touch
       and refreshingly fragrant.
       Henceforth both have the same virtue,
       and the same love (the Beloved's)
       and the same delight:
       "My delight
       is to be with the children of men" (Pr. 8:31).
       "In flower,"
       because the virtues of the soul
       are now perfect and heroic.

Theme: The Bridegroom communicates His own love and His own virtues, with peace and tranquillity.

Note: Stanzas 24–33 correspond to Stanzas 15–24 in the First Redaction.

1.   In speaking of the "bed in flower" there is a definite suggestion of the nuptial bed, which the Saint hastens to describe as "Divine, pure, and chaste"; it is the Bridegroom himself. Reclining there, we too become "Divine, pure, and chaste," divinized, purified, chastened in this loving relationship with the Son of God, in whom is Divine odor and fragrance and grace and beauty.

2–3. Here is another figurative expression of the total giving of self of the Bridegroom: He gives "His breast and His love." To the beloved disciple John, Jesus gave His breast at the Last Supper, and all knew then that John was specially beloved, the "disciple whom Jesus loved." Jesus communicates "His wisdom, secrets, graces, virtue, gifts"; there is nothing more to give. Both have, henceforth, the same virtues, the same love, the same delight; as Jesus' virtues were perfect, heroic, so now are our virtues, which are His, not our own.

4.   *"bound with dens of lions"*:
        The second property of this union.
        Protected by "dens of lions,"
        the strength of the perfect virtues,
        the very properties of God.
        Thus fortified,
        at rest upon this bed in flower
        of union with the Beloved,
        she is so exalted and courageous
        that the devils fear her
        as much as they fear the Beloved.
        The devil has extraordinary fear
        of the perfect soul.

5.   *"bound . . . dens"*:
        Because the virtues are so bound together
        as to have no weakness.
        Not only can the devil find no entry,
        but nothing in the world
        can disquiet, molest,
        or even move the soul.
        She is in security, quietude.
        She participates in God;
        Hence Cant. 8:1:
        "Who will give you to me
        for my brother,
        nursed at the breasts of my mother,
        that I may find you alone outside
        and kiss you,
        and no one despise me?"

        This kiss
        is the union of which we are speaking,
        in which the soul is made equal to God,
        through love.
        All her natural imperfections destroyed
        (received from her mother Eve),
        she wishes to be united to Him alone.
        Thus none will attack her,
        neither the world, nor the flesh, nor the devil.

4. These strong virtues offer a protection from the devil. As Christ put him to flight in the desert, now we too become invulnerable; the strength of these virtues makes us courageous, and it is the devil's turn to be afraid.

5. At last we have found security. With St. Teresa we can truly say, "Let nothing disturb you, nothing disquiet you; God alone suffices." Cf. Ephesians 6:10–20, which is an apt commentary on this state of the soul. The result of this security is deep peace, an habitual sweetness and tranquillity which is never lost and never fails. Cf. St. Teresa's description of this state of peace: "In this Seventh Mansion, the soul seems subject to none of the usual movements of the faculties and imagination, which injure it and take away its peace". The faculties and senses and passions are not always in this state of peace, but the soul itself is. "Nothing enters the soul to disturb its peace . . . the center of the soul is not touched or disturbed; there the King dwells" (I.C. Mans. VII.2).

    The word "security" ("*seguridad*"): St. John uses it in the Latin sense of "*securus*," meaning "free from care or anxiety," not in the sense that we have absolute security about our eternal salvation. St. Teresa reminds us that even in this exalted state "the soul may seem to give the impression that it is sure of salvation . . . this is not so . . . it is sure of itself only insofar as it knows God is holding it by the hand" (I.C. Mans. VII.2). This is the perfection of the virtue of hope; its meaning: no hope in ourselves, complete hope in God.

6.   Even though
        the soul is filled with perfect virtues,
        she is not always enjoying them actually,
        even though she ordinarily does enjoy
        the peace and tranquillity they cause.
        They are present as flower buds in a garden,
        and sometimes, through the Holy Spirit,
        they open to diffuse
        a marvellous variety of fragrance.

7.   *"bed . . . hung with purple"*:
        That is, with charity, that of the King of Heaven.
        By Him
        all the virtues, riches, and goods flourish.
        (cf. Cant. 3:9–10). Charity orders
        and is the means of all the virtues—
        charity of both God and the soul.

8.   *"built up in peace"*:
        The virtues produce in the soul
        peace, meekness, and fortitude.
        Neither the world nor the flesh nor the devil
        can destroy them.

9.   *"and crowned with a thousand shields of gold"*:
        The virtues are flowers,
        but also they are like strong shields
        against the vices (cf. Cant. 3:7, 4:4).

6. A certain qualification of the previous statement regarding the virtues: they are, in fact, really given, but that is not to say that they are habitually enjoyed; in this life it is impossible that this should always be so. This means that to some extent we always feel the burden of the weakness of our human nature. "Sometimes our Lord leaves such souls to their own nature," says St. Teresa, "but only for a short time" (I.C. Mans. VII.4). Only in heaven do the virtues, really present, come to full flowering. Here below they are as flower buds, not fully perfect. Nevertheless it does happen that through the grace of the Holy Spirit they are sometimes in evidence, and then the real holiness of the person shines through. We catch occasional glimpses of this true holiness in certain chosen souls, and it is like the opening of a flower, diffusing its fragrance.

7. Charity, the queen of the virtues, orders and gives life and meaning to all the other virtues. They have meaning only in terms of love of God, drawing their inspiration and meaning from love, and they have love for their goal. A word of warning, though: while it is in a certain sense true to say that "the only thing that matters is love", this should be understood as love supported by the other virtues.

8–9. The two apparent contraries, meekness and fortitude, result from the presence of the virtues. Peace is now enjoyed habitually. St. John suggests that this is caused by the presence of the virtues.

Introduction

1.   The soul here extols
      the excellence of the Beloved
      in bestowing His flowers on other souls.

      "Following your footsteps
      maidens run along the way;
      at the touch of a spark,
      the spiced wine,
      flowings from the balsam of God."

Commentary

2.   The soul enumerates the three benefits
      devout souls receive from the Beloved:
      sweetness, by which they run
      along the road to perfection;
      a visit of love or touch of the Beloved,
      inflaming them;
      and abundance of charity,
      the inebriation of the Holy Spirit,
      in which they burst forth
      in praise and love of God.

Theme: The benefits devout souls receive from the Beloved—Divine touches, inebriation of the Holy Spirit.

1.   The graces received make us more sensitive to the gifts of God that we recognize in others. In fact, persons in this state will readily recognize a kindred spirit, one who is "running in the way" as they are.

2.   "Sweetness" can be a misleading word, as though all is now sweetness and light without suffering. Not so; this sweetness is a sharing in God, which He gives them of Himself and it is of such efficacy that it makes them run quickly in the way of perfection. The effects of the second and third gifts of charity are to praise God for His goodness in others (a mark of true holiness).

3.   "*Following your footsteps*":
         God's sweetness and knowledge—
         the trace by which the soul
         goes on searching for Him.

4.   "*maidens run along the way*":
         Devout souls "run" the way
         according to the spirit God gives,
         in the path of evangelical perfection,
         in many different ways.
         Compare Cant. 1:3: "Draw me,
         we will run after thee
         in the odor of thy ointments."
         Also Ps. 118:32:
         "I have run the way of your commandments
         when you enlarged my heart."
         The soul does very little
         or nothing of her own
         in order to advance along this road;
         rather she is "drawn,"
         moved, and attracted by the Divine footprint
         to go out, to run along the way.

3–4.   Those who receive this special knowledge of God (footprints)
       are "drawn, moved, and attracted" to run along the way of
       perfection, which is love. The favorite "aspiration" of St. Thérèse
       of Lisieux, at the end of her life, and perhaps her only one,
       was simply "Draw me; we will run after thee" (cf. Asc. II.26
       and I.C. VII.3). This was, for her, sufficient prayer for others,
       for those she wished to pray for. "Draw me": the initiative is
       God's. In the Psalm quoted, "I have run the way . . . when you
       enlarged my heart," the same thought comes through. St. John
       reminds us that "the soul does very little or nothing of her
       own." No room for pride; we are drawn, attracted by God, by
       the Divine "footprint" of His gift of this precious knowledge
       of Himself, which precedes His gift of love. Then, we do not
       merely walk; we "run in the way."

5.   *"at the touch of a spark,*
       the spiced wine,
       flowings from the balsam of God":
       Not only in external works,
       but in the interior exercise of the will,
       she runs in the way,
       inflamed by the hot spark or touch
       from the fire of Divine love,
       enkindling the will
       to love, desire, praise, and thank God.
       These acts are *"flowings from the balsam of God."*

5.   The first two lines explain how we "run in the way" by spiritual exercises and external good works, which will always result from this experience (cf. I.C. Mans. VII.4) "This is the purpose of the Spiritual Marriage, of which are born good works and good works alone." These lines deal with the inward movement of the will, which, enkindled by the "hot spark," or Divine touch, of God, is immediately moved to love, desire, praise, and give thanks to God.

These Divine "touches" are important; ecstasies, raptures, visions are not necessary, but it seems that these "Divine, substantial touches" always take place in some way, to suddenly enkindle, as with "the touch of a spark," or as "spiced wine", so that we are immediately inflamed with love of God. These leave a feeling of great comfort and consolation, hence are like balm, or balsam, flowing from God to comfort and console us. Cf. Stanzas 14, 15, paragraph 14. St. John of the Cross deals with the "substantial touches" in *The Ascent* II. ch. 26 paras 3–10. He describes them as "a touch of knowledge and delight that penetrates the very substance of the soul, in which God Himself is experienced and tasted." They can be received only by a person who is already detached and in union with God.

So enriching is the experience, that one of these touches could remove all imperfections, filling the soul with virtues and blessings, more than compensating for all the trials and sufferings of this life. They occur when we least expect them; they can vary in intensity, but the faintest touch of this Divine knowledge, which may occur from simply hearing or repeating some word of Scripture, is more profitable for our spiritual life than many kinds of acquired knowledge. While remaining at peace about whether they occur or not, since they are totally God's doing, we should not behave negatively or try to reject them as we do with other kinds of supernatural occurrence. They are a sure sign of deepening union with God and an indication of His special love.

6.   Compare Cant. 5:4: "My lover
      put his hand through the opening,
      and my heart trembled at His touch."
      The touch of the Beloved is in the will,
      the hand, or favor, being given
      according to the manner of perfection
      in the heart, or will,
      as her desires and affections rise toward God.

7.   *"the spiced wine"*:
      This is the special inebriation of the Holy Spirit
      given to advanced souls,
      their love being fermented and established,
      spiced with the virtues already gained.
      Not only are there greater outpourings of love,
      praise, and adoration of God,
      but also the soul has admirable desires
      to work and suffer for Him.

8.   This favor of inebriation,
      unlike the "spark,"
      usually lasts for a long while,
      sometimes for days,
      though not always
      with the same degree of intensity.
      Compare Ps. 38:4:
      "My heart grew hot within me,
      and in my meditation
      a fire shall be enkindled."

9.   We see here
      the difference between fermented,
      or old wine, and new wine.

6.   This paragraph is a commentary on the quotation from the
       Canticle of Canticles, and the Saint notes that the intensity of
       the "touch," or visit, varies with the spiritual quality of the soul
       (according to the perfection, or maturity, which it has achieved).
       It is the will that is touched, or inflamed.

7.   The "spiced wine" is a special inebriation of the Holy Spirit,
       reserved for those whom St. John calls "*aprovechados,*" or the
       "proficient"—those who have made great progress. This wine
       is the love which is being prepared for them. It is "spiced"
       with the virtues, so that the praise, love, and adoration which
       result are strengthened with great desires to work and suffer
       for God. Cf. I.C. VII. 3: St. Teresa constantly reminds us that
       this desire for trials and suffering will always be the sign of
       the person who really loves God. "Do you know when people
       become really spiritual?" she asks. It is "when they become
       the slaves of God and are branded with His sign, which is
       the sign of the Cross."

8.   In contrast to the "spark", which is momentary, (although its
       effects remain), the inebriation of the Holy Spirit, which is the
       "spiced wine," lasts for some considerable time. The effects
       of the "spark", though, are more ardent; inebriation is a serene,
       tranquil, lasting experience.

9.   New wine is not good for the health; fermentation is still going
       on. Old wine, already fermented, does not spoil or go bad;
       it is pleasant to the taste, and is good for the health.

10.   New lovers, beginners in the service of God,
        are new wine.
        The lees of the weak and sensory part,
        not yet fermented,
        cannot fortify the soul,
        which finds its strength
        in the savors and sweetness of sensory taste.
        This love is imperfect, untrustworthy;
        this new wine of love may easily fall
        and lose its fervor and delight;
        but it can also incline one
        to good and perfect love,
        as a beneficial means
        through the thorough fermentation
        of the lees of imperfection.
        These "new lovers" should drink moderately,
        not letting themselves be carried away
        by the anxieties and fatigues
        of the new wine of their love,
        until there is complete fermentation.

11.   By contrast, the old lovers,
        tried and exercised in the service of the Bridegroom,
        the lees of their wine being fermented,
        have none of the sensitive effervescence
        nor the external fires of the beginners;
        they have the substance, now well fermented,
        of a love based, not on sensible delights,
        but on true spiritual savor within the soul
        and truly good works.
        These souls are careful
        not to indulge sensory taste or fervor,
        lest weariness and distaste overtake them.
        These souls have none of the anxiety
        or affliction of love.
        They hardly ever fail God,
        for they are above sensuality.

10.   New lovers, or beginners in the spritual life, like new wine,
       are not yet tested; they tend to seek gratification in the senses,
       seeking for spiritual consolations, the "lees" of imperfect wine.
       This stage of sensible desires and yearnings for love is passed
       through. This gives way, just as fermentation eventually ceases,
       to stronger desires, centered not in the desire for sweetness
       and consolation but in a stronger love—in faith, centered on
       God alone. Moderation is recommended to those who are still
       in "fermentation," the imperfect; they should not let themselves
       be "carried away." They could mistake the "fermentation"
       experience for genuine mystical experience; a false mysticism
       may result in over-anxiety, undue fatigue, in pursuing
       "experience" for its own sake, with the subsequent loss of
       everything of value.

11.   Those who have made solid progress, however, are not carried
       away by sensible consolations, if they should occur, nor do
       they desire them; the true spiritual favor is "unfelt" in the senses.
       The spiritual savor or sweetness is real, but it is "within the
       soul" and has the ring of authenticity. It is proved by good
       works flowing from a life based on faith ("*Sabor de espiritu
       o verdad de obra*"). Cf. I.C. Mans. VII.4: "This is the aim of
       prayer; this is the purpose of the Spiritual Marriage, of which
       are born good works and good works alone . . . Our good
       resolutions in prayer must be borne out in good works."
       Paragraphs 10 and 11 are a kind of digression—"a little
       instruction for spiritual persons," as St. John says.

Introduction

1. The bride in this happy state can now say,
    "His left hand is under my head."
    She is clothed with God
    and bathed in divinity
    in the interior of her spirit,
    and she experiences the words of Ps. 35:
    "They shall be inebriated
    with the plenty of your house;
    and you will give them to drink
    of the torrent of your delights,
    because with you
    is the fountain of life."
    The torrent is the Holy Spirit,
    a "resplendent river of living water
    which flows from the throne of God
    and the Lamb" (Ap. 22:1).

    "In the inner wine cellar
    I drank of my beloved, and when I went abroad,
    through all this valley
    I no longer knew anything
    and lost the flock which I was following."

Commentary

2. Two effects of this union are here noted:
    forgetfulness or withdrawal
    from all worldly things,
    and mortification of all appetites
    and gratifications.

Theme: Transformation in God in the substance of the soul; the action of the Holy Spirit, bringing about complete detachment.

1. "Clothed with God and bathed in divinity"—but, note, "in the interior of her spirit." "All the beauty of the King's daughter is within" and as the union with God deepens, and the Holy Spirit intensifies His action in the person, less and less (not more and more) is this action apparent outwardly. If, previously, as in the spiritual betrothal, there were raptures, ecstasies, flight of the spirit, and so on, now these cease, almost completely. "The astonishing thing," St. Teresa says (I.C. Mans. VII.3), "is that in this state raptures hardly every occur." Inebriation, drinking of "the torrent," "fountain of life," have scriptural overtones and almost always refer to the Holy Spirit (cf. Jn. 4:14; 7:37–39). Now it is not a river only; we are given to drink of a "torrent of delights," the fullness of the spirit.

2. What was attained in the early stages by dint of great effort now follows, we might say naturally, as an effect of the Holy Spirit's action: detachment and mortification (cf. I.C. Mans. VII.3).

3.   *"In the inner wine cellar"*:
It will be necessary here
that the Holy Spirit
guides the pen of the writer.
The wine cellar is the last
and most intimate degree of love
in which the soul can be placed in this life.
There are seven of these degrees,
or wine cellars, of love.
They are all possessed
when the seven gifts of the Holy Spirit
are possessed perfectly
according to the soul's capacity to receive them.
Thus the degree of filial fear
corresponds to the degree of love.

4.   Many people enter the first wine cellar,
each according to their degree of perfection in love,
but few in this life
reach the last and most interior,
Spiritual Marriage.
This union cannot be put it into words,
As God Himself
cannot be described in words;
it is a transformation
of the soul in God,
in which God communicates himself,
transforming the soul into himself
and communicating His own glory.
In this transformation
the two become one,
as the window united with the ray of sunlight,
the coal with the fire,
the starlight with the light of the sun.
This union is not as essential or perfect
as in the next life.

3.   The Saint indicates that in dealing with these matters we are treading on holy ground, and he feels the necessity of the guidance of the Holy Spirit. It should be remembered that, even though St. John of the Cross had experienced all that he is describing, only by a special grace of God can he put it into words, and set it down in writing.

The seven degrees, or "wine cellars," correspond to the seven gifts of the Holy Spirit. Not that they are received in their perfection one after the other; like the virtues, they "go together," and the degree of each gift corresponds to the degree of love. The Saint takes filial fear merely as an example.

4.   The last wine cellar is the Spiritual Marriage. This union is indescribable, even as God is; the transformation of the person into God can be described only in terms of metaphor, but each metaphor is carefully chosen. The window, the coal, the starlight, remain themselves with their own identity, but are so united with the ray of light, the fire, and the light of the sun, respectively, that all seem to become as one, indistinguishable one from the other. Yet even this union is imperfect compared with that of heaven.

191

5.   *"I drank of my Beloved"*:
This transformation is like a drinking of God
in the substance and spiritual faculties.
With the intellect,
she drinks wisdom and knowledge;
with the will, sweetest love;
with the memory, refreshment and delight
in the remembrance and the feeling of glory.
Compare Cant. 5:6: "My soul delighted as soon as the Bridegroom spoke."
This is the first degree,
the soul drinking delight substantially.

6.   In the second,
the intellect drinks wisdom.
Cf. Cant. 8:2: "There you will teach me
wisdom and knowledge and love,
and I shall give you
a drink of spiced wine."

7.   In the third, the will drinks love:
"He put me in the secret cellar
and set in order charity in me" (Cant. 2:4).
The Bridegroom infuses
His very own love into her.

5–7.   This is a repetition of the Saint's teaching that the transformation takes place in the substance or inner being of the soul. This is the thing to grasp—there is a total transformation. The soul, or the person (which has been the meaning throughout of "soul"), becomes something other in its innermost being, sharing the very nature or being of God. And because the soul is changed, while retaining always its own identity, its powers or operations change—are transformed—too. The powers of the soul, intellect, will, and memory undergo a real transformation, each one acquiring a sharing in God, according to its particular capacity to receive.

Thus to the intellect is given wisdom and knowledge of God; to the will, love: "The Bridegroom infuses His very own love into her." The memory, stripped of any remembrance or attachment to anything other than God, now dwells in refreshment and delight in the new experience of the very glory of God.

One might say of this that it is a mere repetition of what has been said many times before—namely that the soul is transformed into God. But note that St. John of the Cross, skilful teacher that he is, always adds something important to teaching and truths previously enunciated or formulated. He tends to teach in concentric fashion, rather than linear: our knowledge of a truth is gradually enriched and gradually completed; it is not fully stated or exhausted at once. The same truths are presented in many different ways. St. John's Gospel is an example of this.

8.   It is to be remembered
      that supernaturally God can infuse love
      without the infusion of particular knowledge.
      Therefore, one can love greatly
      but understand little.
      In such souls
      infused faith suffices for their knowledge.
      In the case we are describing
      all three faculties drink together.

9.   In the fourth, the memory is illumined
      with intellectual light
      in remembrance of the goods
      the soul possesses and enjoys
      in this union.

10,11. *and when I went abroad*":
      That is, when this favor had passed.
      For even though the soul
      is always in this sublime state
      of Spiritual Marriage,
      once placed there by God
      the faculties are not always in actual union,
      though the substance is.

8.   Here is practical teaching, bearing on our daily experience.
        Can unlettered people love God in the way we are describing,
        even though they have no knowledge in a literary way—"par-
        ticular knowledge" (*text*)—of the truths, we are considering?
        The answer is clear in this paragraph. In showing that "God
        can infuse love without the infusion of particular knowledge"
        the Saint explains that particular knowledge refers to the
        acquired, natural knowledge of these matters; the knowledge
        God infuses is of quite another order and has nothing to do
        with the ordinary learning processes.

        Faith, which God gives, is knowledge, of a different kind and
        dimension, but knowledge indeed. With Abraham mankind
        moved into a new mode of existence; man was able to know
        in a new way; to know God, and communicate with Him, person
        to Person. This is a supernatural knowledge, that of faith, finding
        its expression in love (Gal. 5:2). In the natural order it is
        impossible to love without first perceiving and having
        knowledge of the person or object to be loved.

9.   The memory is cleansed, or dispossessed of hope of pleasurable
        attachments, being supernaturally enlightened as to their true
        worth in the perspective of what is now hoped for, with certainty.

10–11. A distinction is made—one of practical importance. What has
        been said about "habitual union" in this state applies to the
        substance of the soul. That means that in reality the person
        enjoys uninterrupted union with God in the deepest recesses
        of his being, in the "center" of the soul; but the faculties, or
        powers, of the soul—the intellect and will—are not so com-
        pletely possessed by God that they cannot act in a normal
        way. They are not always in actual union; otherwise, it would
        seem impossible that we could perform ordinary, everyday tasks
        and live a normal life. So, when we read of St. Teresa that
        for the last ten years of her life she was in uninterrupted union
        with the Blessed Trinity, we must keep in mind that she
        appeared, and was, a perfectly normal person to those around
        her—more so, in fact, because at this stage such things as
        raptures, visions, had practically ceased. St. Teresa explains
        this in *The Interior Castle* (I.C. VII.2).

12.   *"through all this valley"*:
That is, the world.

13.   *"I no longer knew anything"*:
In drinking of this highest wisdom,
she forgets all worldly things,
so that everything she has ever known
is pure ignorance.
Cf. 1 Cor. 3:19: great wisdom in the sight of men
is foolishness before God.
Cf. Prov. 30:1–2: "And being comforted
by God's dwelling within him,
he said:
'I am the most foolish of men,
and the wisdom of men is not with me.'"
Cf. 1 Cor. 2:14: The high things of God
are foolishness and madness to men.

14.   The soul is so carried out of itself
in this transformation in God
that she can have attention
to no worldly thing,
like the spouse in the Canticle:
"I did not know" (Cant. 6:11).
In a way, she resembles Adam
in the state of innocence,
who did not know evil.
She is so innocent
as to not understand evil,
nor does she judge anything to be bad.
She no longer has within herself
the habit of evil
by which she sees and hears,
since she shall have the perfect habit
of true wisdom.

12–13. All the knowledge that St. Thomas Aquinas had acquired of God during his lifetime seemed "so much straw" when he experienced the Spiritual Marriage. Now we know God as He knows himself; we want no other knowledge, as St. Paul said, but "Jesus Christ and Him crucified" (1 Cor. 2:2). Everything else is "pure ignorance." The Spirit within us "searches out the deep things things of God" (1 Cor. 2:10). Conversely, these deep things of God, and this new life in God of the Spiritual Marriage, seem but foolishness to those who cannot understand.

14.   This paragraph has interesting practical implications. It certainly does not mean that in this state we wander about in a dream world, unable to concentrate on anything mundane. Rather, these "worldly things" are seen in their perspective—as passing, transient. We cannot become absorbed in them, or feel over-anxious or disturbed when things go wrong. "God along suffices . . . all things pass." Another characteristic of truly holy people is mentioned: a certain innocence—an inability to judge or condemn anything or anybody. The "perfect habit of true wisdom" makes it impossible to pass judgement on others, although of course the capacity to recognize what is objectively right and wrong is heightened. Our Blessed Lady must have been supremely charitable in this way. Cf. St. John of the Cross' "Cautions," 3, 8.

15.   She is unmindful
        of the affairs of others,
        as well as of her own.
        This is a characteristic
        of God's Spirit in the soul:
        He gives her an immediate inclination
        toward ignoring and not desiring
        knowledge of the affairs of others.
        She surely is drawn away from external affairs
        by God's spirit, rather than involved in them.

16.   The knowledge already acquired
        of the natural sciences
        is not lost;
        rather these habits are perfected,
        just as a faint light is not lost,
        but perfected by a stronger light.
        Such, I think, will be the case in heaven,
        though the habits of acquired knowledge
        will not be of great benefit,
        as the just will have more knowledge
        through Divine wisdom
        than acquired knowledge can teach them.

17.   In this absorption of love,
        forms of things, imaginative acts,
        and other apprehensions
        are all lost and ignored.
        She becomes so consonant
        with the simplicity of God
        that she remains pure and empty
        of all forms and imaginative figures,
        in the radiance of simple contemplation.
        In shining on a window,
        the sun makes it look bright,
        so that all stains and smudges
        seem to disappear,
        only to reappear when the sunlight passes.

15.   We can take this as a sign of God's action; it comes from "God's Spirit within the soul"; we do not desire to know or to be involved in the affairs of others, unless it is our duty to be so involved. St. John is very emphatic about this; he knows that unmortified curiosity of this kind is a definite obstacle to progress in the love of God, and that it is all too common in religious life (cf. the Saint's teaching in the "Cautions," 8.)

16.   This emphasizes what has already been stated; in no way is our natural knowledge lessened or weakened by the super-natural knowledge of the things of God we now experience in this state. On the contrary, our natural perception is quickened, perfected. The Saint speculates regarding our knowledge in heaven, and comes to the conclusion that natural knowledge is not diminished there either, but is, as it were, transcended and perfected by the Divine wisdom which is the means of all knowledge in heaven. All knowledge acquired there is in, by, and through God.

17.   St. John says here that "in that absorption of love"—that is, when the soul is absorbed in this way—all natural means of knowing cease. No form, concept, or image is now necessary as the means to knowledge. He suggests that the act of simple contemplation itself cleanses and purifies all these natural forms and ordinary means of knowledge. But when the "act" of contemplation passes, we revert to the ordinary ways of knowing.

18. *"and lost the flock which I was following"*:
Until the soul attains to this state of perfection
there always remains
some little "flock" of appetites,
satisfactions, and other imperfections.
The will is captivated
by small appetites and gratifications,
possessions, or judgements,
and other small things having a worldly savor.
These may be natural,
as eating, drinking, desiring the best;
or they may be spiritual,
like the desire for spiritual gratifications.
In the memory
there may be useless imaginings;
in the four passions,
useless hopes, joys, sorrows, and fears.

19. In the wine cellar
these herds of imperfections
are easily consumed,
till the soul feels free
of all childish likes and trifles
and can say,
"and lost the flock which I was following."

18.   This should be read carefully. The Saint is really reverting to
        the imperfections which troubled us before reaching Spiritual
        Marriage, and showing how they have been overcome. The
        "herd" (of imperfections) is now "lost," or left behind.
        Gratification of the senses, the desire of possessing this and
        that (usually things that are superfluous), passing judgements
        on other people, desiring the best of everything (even though
        we have a vow of poverty!)—these imperfections no longer
        trouble us. More subtle is the temptation to wish for some
        kind of spiritual gratification. While these things remain, we
        can be sure, after reading this paragraph, that we still have
        some way to go on the royal road!

19.   "Childish trifles" (*"niñerias de gustillos y impertinencias"*) the
        Saint calls these things; but they are "consumed" and we are
        now free, truly liberated, mature.

Introduction

1.   In this union
God communicates himself
with such genuine love
that no mother's affection
can be compared to it.
Here the soul experiences
the wonder of God's tenderness,
and His humility and sweetness
in, as it were, becoming her slave.
As in the Gospel, girding himself,
and passing from one to the other,
He ministers to them (Luke 12:37).
He favors and caresses the soul
like a mother who ministers to her child,
nursing it at her breasts.
Cf. Is. 66:12: "You shall be carried
at the breasts of God
and upon His knees
you will be caressed."

2.   The soul
makes a complete surrender of herself;
like the bride in the Canticle, 7:10–12:
"there I will give you my breasts."

"There he gave me his breast;
there he taught me a knowledge, very sweet,
and I gave myself to him,
withholding nothing;
there I promised to be his bride."

Theme: God's communication of himself in tenderness and love; mutual surrender.

1. "O marvellous thing and worthy of all awe and wonder. So profound is the humility and sweetness of God!" So exclaims St. John (*text*) in reflecting on the "tenderness and reality of the love wherewith the boundless Father (*"immenso Padre"*) caresses and exalts this humble and loving soul." It is evident from the enthusiam and wonder in this passage that he is speaking from his own experience of the sweetness, the tenderness of God, His humility, His condescension; as with a mother's loving care; "we shall be carried at the breasts, and caressed on His knees"—a favorite passage of St. Thérèse of Lisieux.

2. The keynote of this stanza is "complete surrender," under the symbol of the giving of His breast, of the first line (*"Allí me dio su pecho"*). And the remarkable thing is that St. John has reversed the order, if one may say so, of the Canticle as quoted. "There *He* gave *me* His breast"; the one making the complete surrender is God. This surrender of God, "this breast of God opened to it with such wide and sovereign love," leads us on to a like surrender of our own will and love, and the union is complete. "I will give the strength of my will in the service of your love"—not simply the enjoyment of this intimate love-experience, but giving of myself in service, since this must be the first fruits of this loving union.

Commentary

3.   This is the mutual surrender
        between the soul and God
        which was made in the spiritual betrothal.

4.   *"There He gave me His breast"*:
        God gives His love and His secrets to the bride.

5.   *"There He taught me a knowledge, very sweet"*:
        The secret knowledge of God,
        mystical theology, contemplation,
        which is a delightful knowledge, through love.
        God communicates this knowledge and understanding
        in the love with which He communicates himself
        to the soul.
        This knowledge consists in love,
        which pertains to the will.

6.   *"and I gave myself to Him,
        withholding nothing"*:
        In the desire to be totally His,
        the soul is experiencing God's gift
        of the purity and perfection
        necessary for complete surrender.
        He makes her entirely His own,
        emptying her of all she possesses
        other than himself.
        Here is the fidelity and stability
        of an espousal.

3–4. Not only His love, but His secrets; the ultimate proof of love. References to the spiritual betrothal in Stanzas 26 to 29 have led some to believe that the Saint is dealing only with betrothal, not Spiritual Marriage, in these two stanzas. See also commentaries 7 and 8, below.

5. The "science" or "living knowledge", St. John calls "mystical theology", a term he uses elsewhere to signify infused contemplation (cf. Asc. II.8.6; III.30. 5; D.N. II.5.1 etc.). In the prologue to *The Spiritual Canticle* he says, "Although you lack the knowledge which comes from a study of scholastic theology, by which one comes to an understanding of Divine truth, you are not lacking in mystical knowledge, which is acquired by love". In this paragraph, he is saying that this knowledge consists in love, and it is through love that this "secret, Divine wisdom" is acquired. Cf. D.N. II.17.2.

6. Note that the purity and perfection required for this total surrender of self comes from God; the Saint never wearies of reminding us of this. The small efforts made at detachment in the earlier stages of the journey (Active Night of the Senses and Spirit) are rewarded; it is not now we ourselves who bring about detachment by our own efforts, but God, who "empties us of all we possess other than himself." Now there is stability; there will be no desire to revert to our former state of weakness; we have now something of the fidelity of God himself. "God is faithful"; He never goes back on His promises. St. Paul could say with utter certainty and assurance, "Now I know in whom I have believed" (2 Tim. 1:12).

7.   *"There I promised to be His bride"*:
        The soul is, as it were, deified, Divine;
        no longer does she suffer
        first movements contrary to God's will.
        Cf. Ps. 61:12–13: "Shall my soul
        not be subject to God?
        I shall no longer move."

8.   The soul is now all love;
        all her actions are love;
        she gives up everything,
        like the wise merchant (Mt. 13–44),
        for this treasure of love found hidden in God.
        She no longer esteems anything else but love,
        and neither feels, tastes, nor knows
        the things that happen to her.

7.   This seems to indicate, not marriage, but betrothal; compare
        paragraph 6: "Here is the fidelity and stability of an espousal."
        We sounded a warning earlier not to expect a too rigid adherence
        by the Saint to his own arrangement of verses. While this whole
        group of stanzas (27–31) represents a new "cycle", which is
        more or less repetition of the previous one (17–26), it is
        significant that Stanzas 24 to 35 in the Second Redaction
        correspond to Stanzas 15 to 24 in the First Redaction. This
        means that St. John of the Cross originally considered them
        as applying to the Spiritual Espousal.

        To the end of his life the Saint was reordering and rearranging
        his material, and the result is that we have a more orderly
        and logical, but not definitive, arrangement in the Second
        Redaction. It is not always clear from the text whether he is
        discussing Espousal or Marriage. Nevertheless the whole
        commentary on this verse undoubtedly deals with the Spiritual
        Marriage: "The soul is, as it were, deified, divine" ("*como divina
        endiosada*"). Had we not been prepared for this, we might
        be utterly astonished at this terminology; the word "*deiform*"
        is used in Stanza 39, as we shall see. Something more is now
        added; the effect of becoming "deified" is that there are no
        longer even "first movements" contrary to the will of God.

        We have seen that "first movements," or natural inclinations
        to wrongdoing, are not wilful, and therefore not sinful; the
        "second movements" indicate that the will accepts the wrongful,
        pleasurable thing, and then sin can enter in. Now, united as
        we are to God, even "first movements" toward evil are excluded.
        St. John explains that in the state of imperfection our nature
        turns to what is evil rather than to what is good; now we naturally
        turn to God and to what we know is His will. This, if we realized
        it, is what we pray for in the Our Father: "Thy will be done."

8.   Only love matters now; therefore the passing things of life cannot
        disturb us anymore. In the whole context of the Saint's thought,
        it must be said that he cannot really mean that suffering is
        not "felt"; of course it is, but our reaction to it is one of
        detachment, even joyful acceptance, insofar as we see the hand
        of God in every trial, every vexation, every joy, every satisfaction.

Introduction

1.   The reason why God makes use
of nothing other than love
is that all our works and trials,
even the greatest,
are nothing in His sight.
His only desire is the exaltation of the soul,
and these works can do nothing to attain this.
Only in love can God so exalt the soul
as to make her equal to himself.
Love makes the lover equal
with the object of his love.
The term "bride" signifies equality—
equality with the Son of God.
The possessions of both are held in common.
Cf. John 15:15: "I have now called you my friends,
because all that I have heard from my Father
I have made known to you."

"Now I occupy my soul
and all that I possess in serving him;
I no longer tend the flock,
nor have I any other work
now that I practice love, and that alone."

Theme: Love equalizes; love alone achieves surrender; habitual and loving attentiveness to God's will.

1. Although St. John does not quote chapter 13 of First Corinthians, the Introduction could be a commentary on this classic passage from St. Paul on love: "If I give all I have to the poor, if I deliver my body to be burned and have not charity, I am nothing." No works or trials have any meaning in the sight of God unless they are done in love, out of love. In themselves they are valueless. On the other hand, when done out of love, they are of as great value as love itself, and as we have seen, love must find its expression in works.

    True love equalizes lover and beloved; the Bride is infinitely exalted by the Divine Bridegroom, with a dignity which has meaning only because of Him. All possessions are now in common. Cf. St. John of the Cross' saying, "The heavens are mine . . . God Himself is mine and for me . . ." ("Maxims," 25).

    The quotation from St. John's Gospel indicates that the Apostles are friends because Jesus has shared with them His most precious possession—the knowledge of the Father. The secret communications of one Divine Person to another are now shared with men. This is the work of the Holy Spirit, His task, His function. Cf. also St. John's Gospel, 17:26: "I have made known to them your name . . . that the love with which you have loved me may be in them, and I too may dwell in them." Love can go no further than this. This is God's meaning of "friendship." Cf. St. Thomas Aquinas' notion of "love of friendship," a totally unselfish love, and love of "benevolence," in which one stands to gain something for self, an imperfect love.

Commentary

2.   The soul is now totally occupied
        in the service of the Bridegroom;
        she has no other manner
        of dealing with God than love.

3.   *"Now I occupy my soul"*:
        That is, the soul and all its faculties
        of intellect, memory, will.

4.   *"And all that I possess in His service"*:
        The sensory part;
        the body with all its senses and faculties,
        the four passions, and natural appetites.

5.   From the first instant,
        all her faculties are employed
        and incline toward God in the first movements,
        even though the soul is not always adverting to this.
        She very frequently works for God,
        and is occupied with Him and His affairs
        without adverting to it.
        The custom and habit
        of acting in this way for God alone
        cause her even to omit
        the fervent acts she used to make
        in beginning some work.

2.   The Saint explains that the bride, having given herself totally
      to the Bridegroom, now describes the "mode and manner" of
      this giving. "The soul is now occupied totally in the service
      of the Bridegroom." This does not mean that we turn aside
      from earthly things to give all our attention only to what directly
      concerns God; rather, everything we do, our daily work and
      activity, becomes God-oriented, done for God out of love for
      Him; we live and move and act and have our being in the
      atmosphere of God at every moment. Cf. I.C. Mans. VII. 1: "Not
      that she is unable to fix her mind on nothing else. On the
      contrary, she . . . is more alert than before in all that pertains
      to the service of God."

3.   Intellect, memory, will, are intent on understanding, loving,
      caring for those things which have to do with the service of
      God, and with pleasing Him.

4.   This applies also to the senses, passions, (or emotions), and
      desires. The "whole man" is directed to God. We "have no
      enjoyment except from God, hope in nothing else but in God,
      no fear except from God, no grief except for Him; and all our
      desires and cares are directed to Him alone" (*text*).

5.   "Even though the soul is not always adverting to this" is an
      important phrase in this paragraph. We become aware that
      whereas before we had to "work" to keep our mind on God,
      to recall His presence, purify our intention, and so on, now
      all that seems unnecessary. In the words of St. Paul, we simply
      "walk in love" (Eph. 5:2); we "walk in Him" (Col. 2:6). So
      "without adverting to it" (*text*) we are totally occupied with
      Him and His affairs; and surprising though it may seem, we
      no longer need to make fervent acts in beginning some work,
      as before.

6.   *"I no longer tend the flock"*:
        I no longer follow my appetites.

7.   *"nor have I any other work"*:
        No unprofitable occupations, as before,
        when I had habitual imperfections
        like useless chattering,
        ostentatiousness, compliments, flattery,
        human respect, trying to impress others.

8.   *"Now that I practice love, and that alone"*:
        Cf. Ps. 58:10: "I shall keep my strength for you."

9.   Henceforth, the exercise of prayer
        and communion with God is love,
        without considerations and methods.

10.   This state of spiritual espousal
        can be described
        as walking in the union of love of God,
        which is an habitual and loving attentiveness
        to the will of God.

6–7.   We find that now we are no longer prone to weaknesses like useless chattering, and so on. We no longer pretend to be anything else than what we are in the sight of God; now, at last, by the grace of God, we really know ourselves. God is so important to us that it would seem ridiculous to pretend to put on airs, to order our lives by what others think of us. In other words, we have arrived at the point of maturity which precludes such childishness.

It is interesting to note that the modern school of psychology based on transactional analysis aims at just this—encouraging us to be ourselves and to cease acting according to the "conditioning" of early years and the artificial conventions and inhibitions which largely direct our daily living, as a result of which we never become completely sincere with one another in our daily personal relationships. The fruit of our love of God is sincerity and truth in our dealings with God, with others.

8.   Do we, then, love God like this, in the measure put forward as possible for us all by St. John of the Cross, so that we can say, "My every act is love"? We can apply the test: How sincere, how truthful, am I as a person—with myself, with others, with God? The answer to this question will be an index of the quality of our prayer life.

9.   We now understand St. Teresa: prayer is loving much, not thinking much or relying on "set methods"; an attitude of mind and heart, and this without too many considerations—"the whole thing does not consist in thought" (cf. *Foundations*, chapter 5). St. John adds, "So whether it is dealing with temporal things or spiritual things, it is concerned with love alone."

10.   A state of continual, uninterrupted prayer; an "habitual and loving attentiveness of the will to God" (*Común y ordinaria asistencia de voluntad amorosa en Dios"*). It is not intermittent, as before; now it is habitual, uninterrupted; this is the note of espousal.

213

Introduction

1. The soul is lost to all things,
    and no longer occupies her spirit
    in anything else but love.
    She even withdraws from the active life
    and exterior occupations
    for the sake of the "one thing necessary"
    (Lk. 10:42)—that is, attentiveness to God
    and continual love of Him.
    Cf. Cant. 3:5: the Bridegroom conjures
    all creatures not to hinder
    the bride's spiritual sleep, or love.

2. Until the soul reaches this state,
    she should practice love
    in both the active and contemplative life.
    Yet, once she arrives,
    she should not become involved
    in other works and exterior exercises
    that might be of the slightest hindrance
    to the attentiveness of love toward God;
    even though the work be of great service to God.
    For a little of this pure love
    is more precious to God and the soul
    and more beneficial to the Church,
    even though it seems one is doing nothing,
    than all these works put together.

Theme: Pure love, not activities, is important to God; total withdrawal in nakedness of spirit.

1.   This passage is really a commentary on Our Lord's own words, in Luke 10:42. "Mary has chosen the better part . . . one thing is necessary." It may seem extreme that St. John should suggest that "we withdraw from the active life for the sake of contemplation." He refers, of course, to an active life in which there is so much activity as to make life of intensive union with God difficult it not impossible; over-involvement in active apostolate seems incompatible with a contemplative life; though if charity or obedience requires this activity in the service of the neighbor, St. John would be the last to suggest that it should be abandoned (cf. St. Teresa's *Foundations*, chapter 5).

    It is the activity that is sought for its own sake which is detrimental to a life of prayer; nevertheless if one has the choice, all other things being equal, one should opt for less activity, or withdraw from it altogether, if there is to be "attentiveness to God and continual love of Him." In other words, the contemplative life in itself is more readily conducive to recollection and prayer than the purely active life; but one can be a person of great action, and a real contemplative too.

    Those who feel the call to a more intensive prayer life should follow this way if they can; this paragraph and those which follow are the answer to those who regard the purely contemplative life as something of an anachronism, unnecessary in our age of technology and social action. We are brought back to Our Lord's words, "One thing is necessary."

2.   "Until the soul reaches this state . . ."; and then? Must we abandon active works? Yes, the Saint says in his uncompromising way; those works which can in the least prevent the attentiveness of her love toward God" ("*que le puedan impedir un punto de aquella assistencia de amor en Dios*"). Of course, not all active works do this, but the Saint implies that most active works do (because we all tend to become immersed in them). He goes on: ". . . though the work be of great service to God." This seems a hard saying; but let us read on. If we really believe, as St. John does, in the truth of the following sentence, a gem resplendent among sayings of the mystics, then we can accept the Saint's teaching in all its stark forthrightness. "For a little of this pure love is more precious to God and the soul . . . than all these works put together." We find ourselves asking, if we are honest, "Have I even a little of this pure love?" and "Do I really believe this?"

3.   Great wrong would be done to a person
            who possesses some of this solitary love,
            as well as to the Church,
            if we should urge him to be occupied
            in exterior or active things,
            even if the works are very important
            and demand only a short time.
            Love is the end for which we were created.
            Let those, then, who are very active,
            who think they can win the world
            with their preaching and exterior works,
            observe that they would profit the Church,
            please God, and give good example,
            were they to spend half the time in prayer,
            even though their prayers be not as sublime
            as this we are discussing.
            They would accomplish more,
            with less labor, by one work
            than by a thousand otherwise.
            They would achieve their end
            and be spiritually strengthened.
            Without prayer, they would accomplish little
            and perhaps cause harm.
            May the salt not lose it savor.

3.   Commentary on paragraph 3 seems superfluous. Those whose lives are given over to action could reflect carefully on these words. The message is contemporary; we can't dismiss it by saying that that was "all right in the sixteenth century." We know from the life of St. John that he had exactly the same problem which faces us today, that of ever-recurring strife between extremists on both sides of the action–contemplation controversy. Some of his Carmelite confrères thought to change the world by preaching, to the detriment of their prayer life. The Saint himself carried on quite a full apostolate, mainly of spiritual direction, but the first thing in his life, in keeping with his Carmelite vocation, was prayer, and for him there was no substitute for that.

After all, this paragraph is a simple commentary on the Gospel, and it reflects the teaching and example of Christ Himself; but we all need to be continually reminded of it. Prayer and apostolate must be co-ordinated, and St. John reminds us that apostolate without prayer can actually cause harm.

The message of Vatican II on this point is clear: bishops and priests, especially, are to "share the fruits of their contemplation" with their people (*Decree on the Priesthood*, No. 12), their first duty being "to teach them to pray" (Const. Church No. 45). Religious are to "adhere to God with mind and heart, by contemplation, listening to Christ's words" (*Decree for Religious*, No. 5). The laity are to achieve a "living union with Christ from their daily lives in the world" (*Decree for the Laity*, No. 4). St. John of the Cross does not seem too demanding in these terms!

4.   *"If, then, I am no longer*
         seen or found on the common,
         you will say that I am lost;
         that, wandering love-stricken
         I lost my way, and was found."

Commentary

5.   The soul replies
         to those who criticize her withdrawal,
         judging her conduct useless;
         and even glories in having lost the world
         and given up former worldly pastimes,
         counting this loss as a gain.

6.   *"If, then, I am no longer*
         seen or found on the common":
         "Common"—that is, the world and worldly interests.

7.   *"you will say that I am lost"*.
         Cf. Luke 9:26: "Whoever is ashamed
         to confess the Son of God before men . . ."

8.   Few spiritual persons reach this point
         of losing themselves entirely,
         doing their works for Christ alone
         with complete nakedness of spirit,
         without thought
         as to what others may say or do.

9.   *"that, wandering love-stricken"*:

10.   *"I lost my way, and was found"*:
         Being truly in love,
         she lost herself
         by paying no attention to herself in anything,
         and thinking only of the Beloved;
         she also paid no attention
         to the affairs of others.
         Such is one who is really in love with God.

4–5.   This is a reply to the critics, of whom there are many, and not all of them atheists or irreligious people! They judge "her conduct useless"; she is wasting her time, she should be doing something useful, like teaching Catechism, social work, and so on. Was Mary wasting her time at the Lord's feet?

But at this stage of our journey, this criticism does not disturb us; in St. John's words, we know that "these know nothing of the hidden root and source whence the water springs and whence comes all fruit." We are glad to have "lost the world" in this way, glad to have done with amusements and pastimes which formerly seemed necessary. St. Paul, having discovered Christ, "counted all things as garbage"; "I glory in the Cross of the Lord Jesus Christ; what was formerly loss, is now gain" (Phil. 3:7).

6–7.   The paradox of the Gospel: we are "lost"; but to lose all is to gain all. We lose life to gain it. It is the choice offered us by Christ; this world, or the next.

8.   St. John sadly remarks that there are few of us who reach this point of detachment; or rather, as he says more specifically, "this perfect boldness and determination in their works." We are all so prone to "look at what will be said of us" (*text*); we do not "live truly in Christ"; we are not truly "lost" in the sense of the poem. We are "ashamed to confess the Son of God before men" (paragraph 7). We call it human respect.

9–10.   The Saint, with characteristic realism, says "he that is truly in love ["*el que anda de veras enamorado*"] allows himself to be lost to all things": nothing but love can explain this attitude which seems so "unnatural" to worldly people Reading the autobiography of St. Thérèse, we see that an all-consuming love for God had brought her to this very state of which we are speaking—a holy indifference, an imperturbability even when confronted with the prospect of great suffering, whether spiritual, moral, or physical: ". . . she took no heed of anything pertaining to herself, but only to those concerning the Beloved."

11.   Thus St. Paul says, "to die is gain."
And Our Lord: "He who desires to gain his soul
shall lose it,
and he who loses it for my sake
shall gain it" (Mt. 16:25).
The soul has "lost" all roads and natural methods
in her communion with God,
no longer seeks Him by reflections,
forms, or sentiments,
nor by any other way of creatures or the senses,
enjoying communion with God in faith and love;
then God is her gain.

11.   "Such is one who is really in love with God"—not merely who "loves" but is "in love" (*"enamorado de Dios"*). St. John interprets the passage from St. Matthew—"losing one's life to gain it"—as seeking God by faith and love, and that means seeking Him, in this exalted state of the Spiritual Marriage, in a way which is "purified" of all reflections, imaginations, feelings. For these, he says, are rather obstacles in the way of "having" God as He is. This is possible only by faith—faith, "the only proximate and proportionate means to the understanding by which the soul may attain to the Divine union" (Asc.II 8.9). We need to be reminded of this.

In this life, even the Spiritual Marriage rests on the foundation of faith. We are brought back to the very first stanza: "However sublime our knowledge of God . . . He still remains hidden in the soul." In this life of faith, God is not possessed "essentially"; recall St. Paul to the Corinthians, chapter 13: in this life, we see God "as in a glass, darkly"; but in the next life, when only love remains, we see God "as He is." Faith must always be informed by love; this is "living faith."

Introduction

1.   The Bridegroom and the bride, in mutual exchange of their virtues
and graces each for the other,
celebrate the feast of their espousal,
with wine of savory love
in the Holy Spirit.

"With flowers and emeralds
gathered on cold mornings
we shall we weave garlands
flowering in your love
and bound with one hair of mine."

Commentary

2.   The bride describes the solace and fruition;
each enjoys the virtues and gifts of the other.
This enjoyment of the virtues
is the weaving of garlands.
"With flowers and emeralds":
the soul's virtues and gifts from God.

3.   *"gathered on cold mornings"*:
In time of youth
when the passions are strong.

4.   The "cold mornings" can also mean
those works done in difficulty
and dryness of spirit.
These give greater pleasure to God
than those performed
out of the relish and sweetness
one may experience.
Virtue takes root
in dryness, difficulty, and labor;
"Virtue is made perfect in weakness" (2 Cor. 12:9).

Theme: Mutual exchange of virtues—God and the soul.

1–3. It would be well to read first the whole commentary on this
verse; otherwise we might think that all will be flights of poetic
fancy—flowers, emeralds, garlands, and so on. On the contrary,
St. John (concentric method) is now elaborating on the theme
touched on frequently in previous stanzas: the virtues as gifts
of God. This is all very practical. We notice, with some surprise,
that in the writings of both St. Teresa and St. John, when we
least expect it, and especially when they deal with the higher
stages, they bring us right down to earth. The love of God,
contemplation, the mystical life, is something to be lived out
in the "terrible everyday" of ordinary living; we don't live in
the stratosphere—feet firmly on the ground, please! Understanding "flowers" as virtues, and "emeralds" as the gifts of
God, we can proceed soberly.

4. St. John reminds us in passing that "cold mornings" suggest
to him that the virtues practiced in early years have a special
fragrance, as it is just in these years that the passions are
stronger; and he reflects on the great merit of a life lived entirely
for God from one's youth. It must be said, though, that in the
case of many great Saints this was not so. St. Thérèse, who
probably never offended God seriously, had a special devotion
to St. Mary Magdalen. She realized that her own virtues were
gifts of God, as St. John says here. But the Magdalen's conversion
was His gift to her, too.

5,6.   *"we shall weave garlands"*:
          The virtues and gifts
          which the soul (and God within Her) acquires
          are like a garland,
          woven or fixed firmly in the soul,
          making a garland of perfection.
          Cf. Ps. 44:10: "The queen stood at your right hand,
          clothed in a garment of gold,
          surrounded with variety."
          Note that both weave together.
          The soul cannot practice
          or acquire the virtues
          without the help of God,
          nor does God effect them
          without her help.
          "Every good gift and every perfect gift
          is from above, having come down
          from the Father of lights."
          Yet this gift is not received
          without the ability and help
          of the soul receiving it.
          So the Bride in the Canticle:
          "Draw me, we shall run after you" (Cant. 1:3).

7.   This verse refers also to Christ and His Church.
          Each holy soul in the Church
          is like a garland adorned
          with flowers of virtue and gifts,
          all forming a garland for the head of Christ,
          especially the virgins, doctors, martyrs.

5–6.   Everyone who takes the spiritual life seriously should read and reread this passage. Many good people give up the struggle because they seem to experience nothing but aridity, dryness, difficulty in prayer, apparent failure in virtue, and so on. But St. John's directive is clear. The "difficulty and dryness of spirit" experienced are to be *preferred* to "relish and sweetness." It is a "great leap forward" in the spiritual life when we grasp this, and are prepared and content to live by it.

The virtues we practice at this time, even if we have nothing more to offer to God than the fidelity of going on courageously, with determination, are especially pleasing to God. One could say that courage, generosity, and determination are St. Teresa's favorite virtues; she knows that with these, God will do the rest; without them, He cannot. Take note of St. John's monumental statement, "Virtue takes root in dryness, difficulty, and labor."

A further commentary on the need of our co-operation: not simply "draw me"; that is first, and is necessary, but "we shall run after you." Both God and ourselves work together to make a "garland" of all the virtues; then "the garland of perfection is completed in the soul." Our Lady's "Be it done to me" was necessary to God's plan for our sanctification. We, too, must say "Yes." Like St. Thérèse, we must, like a small child, make the effort to climb on to the first rung of the ladder, or to get up on to the first step of the stairway. God, seeing our effort, like a good father or mother comes down and lifts us in His arms.

7.   It is inevitable that being so closely united with Christ, the Bridegroom, we should have a heightened sense of the Church, which is the Body of Christ. As our love for Christ deepens, so does our awareness of the Church—that is, of our "oneness" with all others who, like us, are integrated into and are one with the glorified Body of the Risen Christ, which is the Church. This is the work of the Spirit. Usually our notion of the Church is too limited; St. John broadens our vision to make us aware of our personal union in Christ with the Church Triumphant, as well as with the Church on earth and the Church in Purgatory. By the holiness, the virtues, and the gifts of God we have come to posses—we form—with all others in heaven, "one garland, for the head of Christ, the Spouse."

8.   *"we shall weave garlands*
flowering in your love":
The works performed
flower only because of love;
without it they wither and are valueless,
no matter how otherwise perfect
from the human point of view.

9.   *"and bound with one hair of mine"*:
This hair is her will,
and love is like the thread of the garland,
binding together.
So love binds and fastens together,
sustaining the virtues in the soul:
"Charity is the bond of perfection."
If this love should break,
by an offence against God,
the virtues would immediately scatter and disappear.
"one hair": because now her will is alone,
detached from other extraneous love.
The virtues become perfect, complete,
and full flowering in the love of God
only so far as love is fixed firmly
on God alone.

10,11. We contemplate the strength
and the beauty of the bride,
mindful of the words of the Canticle,
"How beautiful are your steps,
in sandals, O Prince's daughter,"
denoting her royal inheritance.
Also, "You are terrible,
like an army set in battle array."

8–9. Only love can make these virtues flower, and it is the thread of the garland; it binds and holds together, sustaining and supporting all the virtues. A serious fall from grace, if possible at this stage, would mean that all the virtues are lost. They cannot exist without love, and all stand or fall together.

10–11. St John hastens to say that, in this exalted state, our will— "one hair"—is so detached, so free for God alone, that the garland is perfect, complete in itself. Not only is the work of God in us, the bride, beautiful to contemplate, but there is a formidable strength in the purity and goodness now emanating from us which causes awe in those who see it; like the Blessed Virgin herself, "'terrible as an army set in battle array." We have come into our "royal inheritance."

Introduction

1. "Love is the bond of perfection,"
    which is union with God.
    It is love which binds the bride to God,
    uniting and transforming them,
    each into the other.
    Though they differ in substance,
    in glory and appearance
    the soul seems to be God
    and God seems to be the soul.

2. Compare the love of David and Jonathan,
    whose souls were "knitted" to each other;
    what must the tie be
    which binds Bridegroom and bride
    when God, the lover,
    so binds and absorbs the soul into Himself!

    "That single hair of mine
    waving on my neck has caught your eye;;
    you gazed at it upon my neck,
    and by it captive you were held
    and one of my eyes has wounded you."

3. The soul explains three things:
    that her love is a strong love,
    that God was captivated by the single hair of her love,
    that God was attracted
    by the purity and integrity of her faith.

4. *"That single hair of mine*
    waving on my neck has caught your eye":
    The soul loves with fortitude;
    love, like the hair,
    weaves the virtues together.
    The virtues stand together;
    if one fails, they all fail.
    The breeze of the Holy Spirit
    arouses the strong love
    to produce the effects of the virtues
    present in the soul.

Theme: God is captivated by the soul's faith and virtues, which are the work of the Holy Spirit, yet merited.

1.   What is perfection? "Union with God," says St. John. The theologians say, "Perfection is charity." Both are one and the same thing. It is love which binds the soul to God, so firmly "uniting and transforming them, each into the other (*text*). *El alma parece Dios, y Dios el alma*: The soul *seems* to be, not *is*, God; they "differ in substance, [but] in glory and appearance the soul seems to be God and God seems to be the soul."

2.   A union wondrous beyond expression: the principal lover here is God himself; He absorbs the soul ·in Himself with the omnipotence of His boundless love, with more efficiency and force than that of a torrent of fire absorbing a drop of morning dew. Such is the strength and subtlety of the love that binds ("the hair").

3.   There is some confusion in the translations of the original *no es otro sino solo y amor fuerte*, but in view of paragraph 5 it seems that St. John meant "solitary"—that is, for God alone: "no other love then solitary and strong love." Not only love captivated God, but purity and integrity of faith.

4.   Again and always, the Holy Spirit: "as the breeze stirs the hair upon the neck". The imagery seems to be somewhat complicated, a little strained: "hair" is love; "neck", fortitude; and so on. It is the truth and the doctrine which matter; and the Saint is rigidly orthodox in interpreting what seem rather extravagant flights of poetic imagery, strange to us even when taken directly from Scripture. The "Spirit breathes where He wills"—and in this wonderful experience of Divine intimacy the Spirit is the unseen Mover, the "power behind the scene," love itself, arousing in us that very love which binds us to Jesus, the Bridegroom, and through Him, to the Trinity.

5.   *"you gazed at it upon my neck"*:
       God, seeing the strength of the love in the soul,
       "gazed at"—that is, loved—it.

6.   This love became strong
       through mortifications, trials, penances,
       leading to strong detachment
       from other loves, appetites, and affections.

7.   Hence the soul merits the divine union.

8.   *"and by it captive you were held"*:
       We remember
       that "God first loved us" (1 Jn. 4:10).
       A small bird may capture the royal eagle
       if the eagle desires to be captured.

9.   *"and one of my eyes has wounded you"*:
       The eye of faith—
       she loves with single-hearted fidelity,
       without admixture of human respect.

10.   Cf. Cant. 4:9: "You have wounded my heart, my sister;
       you have wounded my heart
       with one of your eyes
       and with one hair of your neck."

5.   God "beholds" with love, seeing in us a love that is strong—
        and "solitary," single-minded—not weakly turned aside by other
        allurements. Both St. Teresa and St. John emphasize "strength"
        in virtue; St. Teresa tells her nuns "not to be effeminate but
        to be like strong men" in the service and love of God, and
        she certainly showed the way. This love of God requires a
        fortitude even to the point of heroism; not everyone is capable
        of it.

6.   The heroism of mortification, bearing trials of all kinds, doing
        voluntary penance; this demands fortitude—not to commence,
        but to persevere. We might note here that throughout this treatise
        St. John has not put much emphasis on mortifications as such;
        he presupposes the understanding that a basic requirement
        is that we understand that "prayer and self-indulgence cannot
        exist together" (St. Teresa).

7.   The word "merits" is important. God took the initiative, and
        gave all the way; our little efforts, though, are meritorious. We
        have earned the right to something to which by nature we have
        no right at all.

8–10.   "Single-hearted fidelity" ("*esta fidelidad única*") is the key
        phrase, explaining why God, "the royal eagle," allowed Himself
        to be "captivated" from the outset. He *wanted* to be "taken."

Introduction

1.   Those who act with love and friendship toward God
       make Him do all they desire.
       The soul that loves holds God a prisoner.

       "When you looked at me
       your eyes imprinted your grace in me;
       for this you loved me ardently,
       and this my eyes deserved—
       to adore what they beheld in you."

Commentary

2.   The bride is anxious
       that nothing be attributed to her;
       it was His favor in gazing on her
       that transformed her;
       her merit comes from this alone.

3.   *"When you looked at me"*:

4.   *"your eyes imprinted your grace in me"*:
       In His mercy ("eyes")
       God lifts the soul so high
       as to make her a partaker in divinity.

Theme: all is God's doing; nothing is attributed to the soul.

Here commences a group of three stanzas (32–34) describing the soul's intimacy with God.

1. The power of love: we can now "make Him all [we] desire". We are reminded of St. Augustine's "Love, and do what you will." The explanation of that saying is in this paragraph: when we love, we have power over God; He cannot refuse us—but, then, because we love, and our will is His and His ours, we could not want anything but what He wants! The symbolic "exchanging of hearts" of Jesus and the Saints we read about was simply this. We remember Jesus' words to St. Gertrude: "From now on, my will is yours, and yours mine." Cf. Jn. 15:7 and St. Teresa's *Relations*, No. 51. St. John explains further: "Great is the power and the insistence of love, which conquers and binds God Himself . . . His nature is such that those who take Him by love . . . will be able to bring about whatever they wish; there is no other way of influencing God, or interceding with Him."

2. St. John of the Cross explains that in the last two stanzas there seems to be a suggestion on our part of boasting, of "attributing some worth and merit to ourselves." Now we understand clearly that the reason for it all lies in one thing alone: the Bridegroom, Christ, has deigned to look on us, and in that glance we were made "graceful and pleasing in His sight." We are now "worthy to adore our Beloved in a way pleasing to Him"; we are now (note this as the culmination of prayer) "worthy to do works worthy of his grace and love" (*text*). Cf. I.C. Mans. VII.

3. For God to look is for God to love, and to effect some lasting good in us.

4. "Your eyes"—that is, the Bridegroom's "merciful Divinity" gazing on us in merciful love—makes us "sharers in His Divinity."

5.   *"for this you loved me ardently."*
     By infusing His grace into the soul,
     God makes it worthy of His love;
     only thus can the soul merit His grace.
     Jn. 1:16: "He gives grace for grace."

6.   It merits God himself in every act,
     in all her works, because God,
     in loving her, makes her His equal,
     loving her within himself.

7.   *"and this my eyes deserved—*
     to adore what they behold in you":

8.   Previously the faculties were unable
     to look at God;
     now every work becomes meritorious,
     and every act of adoration is meritorious
     and pleasing to the Bridegroom.

9.   The soul in sin,
     unillumined by the love of God,
     is incapable
     of thus ceaselessly adoring and serving God
     with all her faculties;
     she does not even merit
     to look at and know Him.

5. Here is St. John of the Cross' notion of "meriting" God's grace. The first grace, the initiative, is always from God; then, in accordance with Scripture (John 1:16), he gives "grace for grace"; each grace, freely given, "merits" another, as long as we place no obstacle. This thought is more fully developed in the next stanza (in "concentric" fashion).

6. God loves us "within himself." Cf. Our Lord at the Last Supper: "I am in the Father and the Father is in me"; "on that day you will understand that the Father is in me and I am in you" (Jn. 14:10, 20). Then follows what is perhaps the most astonishing statement of all: "So, placed as it is in that lofty state of grace, it merits God himself in its every work."

7-8. Here St. John makes clear what he means by "works." To "behold" Him is to merit to do works "in the grace of God"; and this "work" is to adore God, recognizing and realizing, as never before, His sweetness, His immense goodness, His love, His mercy, all His Divine attributes. "Seeing" God thus in the new intimacy of this loving relationship, we now "merit to adore that which we see in Him."

Note that this new capacity for adoration is a special gift of God—for before this they deserved neither to adore nor to see, such is the blindness of the soul without grace. Do we sufficiently appreciate "adoration" in prayer—that it is a gift of God?

9. A short reflection on the tragic state of the person who is not in the grace of God; the implication is that the grievous affliction is "not meriting to adore"; "the wretchedness of those who live in sin is complete."

Introduction

1.   God's glance
       produces four goods in the soul:
       it cleanses, endows with grace,
       enriches, and illumines.
       It is like the sun which dries,
       and whose rays provide warmth,
       beauty and splendor.
       When God cleanses from sin,
       He no longer remembers her former ugliness;
       He no longer reproaches her,
       since He never judges a thing twice.

       Yet the soul
       should not become oblivious
       of her former sins.
       "Be not without fear for sins forgiven" (Ecclus. 5.5).
       And this for three reasons:
       to have always a motive against presumption,
       to have cause for rendering thanks,
       and to increase her gratitude.

Theme: Contrasts the soul's former state with what God has perfected in her; always the Divine initiative.

1.   The "glance" or the "look" ("*mirada*") of God in the Scriptures has something of the dynamic force of the Word of God. It effect, or brings about, some change in the person; "the Lord looked on Peter" (Lk. 22:61). In the Old Testament we read, "The Lord looked upon my affliction" (Ex. 4:31; Deut. 26:7; etc.). In this state, the Lord has "looked on" us; and it is sufficient for transformation of life.

We have here, in fact, all the effects of "sanctifying grace," for the Lord's glance is the Lord's action to sanctify—to cleanse, to enrich, to enlighten, to renew. And, St. Teresa reminds us, "He never takes His eyes off you." We are reminded that when God cleanses us from sins it is as though they no longer exist; in fact, they do not exist. Yet, we must always retain the spirit of compunction, of genuine repentance for our sinfulness.

There is something mysterious about the insistence of the great Saints on their sinfulness when in fact they were not actually in a state of sin; but the nearer they approached God the better they understood the sinfulness of man as contrasted with that of the Infinite Goodness of God. In the case of St. Teresa, the awareness of sin and the reality of sinfulness in herself and in others is a special, mystical grace. On her death-bed, far from exulting in the great favors she had received from God, she repeated over and over again, "A contrite and humble heart, O God, you will not despise." Cf. I.C. Mans. VII.3: ". . . the more such souls are favored by God, the more fearful they become, being now aware, because of their closeness to God, of the seriousness of their sins and their own wretchedness."

St. John lists three practical reasons why we should not be forgetful of past sinfulness. Note how often we proclaim our sinfulness and need of forgiveness in the prayers of the Mass.

2.   So, aware that in the past
            she was not even worthy
            that God should pronounce her name,
            but that now, because of God's love,
            she merits His favor,
            she boldly requests
            for the continuation of God's favours:

            "*Despise me not;*
            for if before you found me dark
            now truly you can look at me
            since having looked at me
            in me you left your grace and beauty."

Commentary

3.   Previously, when by her unsightliness
            she had rendered herself unworthy
            of the Divine glance,
            He had mercifully deigned to gaze upon her,
            transforming her;
            how much more now
            that she is clothed in His own beauty?
            And He can do so many more times,
            increasing her beauty.

4.   "*Despise me not*":
            Not out of desire or esteem,
            but because of God's gifts and graces.

5.   "*for if before you found me dark*":
            My unworthiness.

6.   "*now truly you can look at me,*
            since having looked at me":
            Now I can merit being seen;
            you have made me worthy.

2.   With this awareness, there is the keen realization that of our-
        selves we can do nothing, have done nothing, to merit God's
        goodness; nevertheless, because of Him, we have merited, and
        this emboldens us to ask Him to continue His favors.

3.   We note how the word "look" (*mirar*) is stressed in the poem.
        One is reminded of Romans 5:3 where St. Paul argues so
        persuasively with the Romans: if God saved, justified, them when
        they were still sinners, how much more now that they are
        reconciled to Him? Similarly here: previously we were "dark"
        (reminiscent of "I am dark, but beautiful," of the Song of Songs);
        now we are clothed with beauty, a beauty not our own, but
        beauty no less radiant than that of the Bridegroom. This beauty
        does not fade—unlike earthly beauty, which is so fleeting. With
        a certain insistence, we remind the Bridegroom that He can
        make us still more attractive if He wishes. "He may well look
        upon her a second time, and many times more."

4–6.   A reaffirmation of the fact that we have merited the
        transformation which has taken place, for God has looked on
        us, "dark" as we were; thenceforth every new gift of God makes
        us worthier in His sight.

7.   *"In me you left your grace and beauty"*:
God gives "grace for grace" (Jn. 1:16).
Moses, knowing this, said:
"If I have found grace in Thy sight,
show me your face
that I may know you
and find grace in your sight" (Ex. 33:12–13).
Now that the soul is in grace,
God loves her,
not as previously, on account of Himself,
but now for her sake too.
So He continues
communicating grace for grace,
becoming continually
more deeply enamored of her.
Thus (Is. 43:4:) Jacob says,
"Because you have become honorable
and glorious in my sight,
I have loved you."
Similarly in the Canticle 1:5
"I am black but beautiful . . .
wherefore the King has loved me
and brought me to His inner chamber."

7.   St. John says, "The more God magnifies the soul, the more does He become captivated by it." As an artist admires his masterpiece, the more perfect it becomes; God becomes more and "more deeply enamored of her." There is food for meditation on the mysterious ways of God in these passages, and St. John of the Cross suddenly lights up passages in the Scripture which previously seemed so puzzling—for example, the Scriptural passages quoted from Exodus, Isaias, and the Song of Songs. Once we accept his explanation of Jn. 1:16, "grace for grace," we can understand his teaching on how we merit God's grace.

8.   This is in accord with the Gospel:
        "To him that has will be given more
        until he abounds,
        and from him that has not,
        even what he has
        shall be taken from him" (Mt. 13:12).

9.   Cf. Esther 6:11:
        "He is worthy of such honor whom the King honors."

8–9.   It is difficult to give a satisfactory interpretation of sayings such as this except against the background of these pages and their explanations by St. John. They have a mystical meaning far beyond their literal sense; indeed a study of St. John of the Cross throws light on many such passages of Scripture. It is hardly possible to read and appreciate the Sacerdotal Prayer of St. John's Gospel (chapter 17) unless one is able to read it in this way, with the awareness of the "mystical" dimension— "mystical" in the sense of pointing to a reality far beyond that conveyed by the apparent, or surface, meaning of the words used. In fact, one could say this of the whole of St. John's Gospel. It has been said (by St. Irenaeus) that only those who have "leant on the Lord's breast" like St. John the Evangelist can understand and appreciate the "spiritual" Gospel. Written by one who was undoubtedly a "mystic" it has been called also the "mystical" Gospel.

The Psalms also yield unsuspected depth of meaning in the light of St. John of the Cross' interpretations, though not all modern exegetes would agree, from a strictly scientific point of view, with some of his "accommodated" meanings and interpretations. Those who have had the experiences described here will understand readily enough. "Mystical wisdom, which comes through love . . . is given according to each one's capacity . . . to accept in Faith" (Prologue).

Introduction

1.   The Bridegroom now praises
        and extols the bride,
        just as she does him.
        Cf. Canticle 1:14: "Behold you are beautiful,
        my beloved, and fair"
        (not black and ugly, as she had said).

        "The small white dove .
        has returned to the ark with an olive branch,
        and now the turtle dove
        has found its longed-for mate
        by the green river banks."

Commentary

2,3.   *"The small white dove":*
        Now white and pure,
        like a dove,
        she is now simple and meek
        in her loving contemplation,
        seen in the brightness of her eyes.

4.   Like the dove which left Noah's ark,
        the soul has returned from the dark waters
        of its sins and imperfection;
        not only cleansed
        by resting on the breast of the Beloved,
        but bearing the olive branch of victory,
        her newly won peace of soul,
        and the reward of her merits.

Theme: The Bridegroom praises the bride's desire for solitude.

1.   This stanza is the reply of the Bridegroom to the protestations of the bride about her unworthiness and past sinfulness. He does not deny this, but makes no reference to it, with the delicacy of love which has forgiven and forgotten. To forget in this way is a Divine quality!

2-3.   The figure of the dove, taken from the Song of Songs, denotes distinguishing marks of really holy people—simplicity and meekness. "Learn of me," Jesus said, "because I am meek and humble of heart."

4.   The olive branch was a sign from God that in His mercy He had at last commanded the waters to recede. The dove, returning with the olive branch, returns to the shelter of God's omnipotence, only there finding solace and rest after its struggle with the "dark waters" of imperfection and sin and separation from Him. Resting on His breast, we can speak of victory, a victory which is in every sense His; but there follows great peace of soul, and the sense of enjoyment of reward, as though the new sense of well-being were really well deserved. Cf. I.C. Mans. VII.3: "God and the soul have fruition of each other in the deepest silence and tranquillity."

5.   *"and now the turtle dove*
        . . . green river banks":
        Like the turtle dove,
        which refuses all comfort
        if it does not find its mate,
        so the soul must advance,
        refusing all satisfactions of the appetites,
        spurning worldly honor and glory,
        or any other affection,
        sighing only for solitude in all things
        until she reaches the fullness of love.

6.   Compare the Bridegroom's words in Canticle 1:2–3:
        "I sat down in the shade
        of Him whom I desired,
        and His fruit was sweet to my palate."
        Now she drinks
        the clear water of contemplation
        and wisdom of God,
        and the cool water of refreshment in Him.

5.   Again, we are reminded that there can be no relaxation of the effort to be virtuous; we must continue to work at the everyday virtues, to practice detachment in ordinary things, and to foster the spirit of recollection. The "turtle dove" must not rest the foot of its desire upon the green bough of any delight, nor desire to taste the coolness of any temporal consolation or refreshment; all this continues to make demands on human nature. And, in the Saint's inexorable fashion, he goes on to speak of desiring in no way to find rest in anything, or find companionship in other affections. On the contrary, there is to be always a sighing after solitude, especially solitude of the heart, even though God may not indulge the desire for physical solitude. It is the desire which is important and, for St. John, a condition and sign of true contemplation.

6.   Having made this point, the Saint hastens to say that with such dispositions we can now say, with a glad heart, that we have truly "arrived"; we now "drink the clear water of the highest contemplation," finding "refereshment and delight in God." "Nothing enters the soul to disturb its peace. The things it hears may cause it distress, but the center of the soul is not touched or disturbed; there the King dwells" (I.C. Mans. VII.2).

Introduction

1.   Now the soul, established in the peace
of solitary love of her Spouse,
has God as her guide,
and needs no other masters or means
to direct her to Him;
He is her guide and her light.
Cf. Osee 2:14: "I shall lead her into solitude
and there speak to her heart."

"She lived in solitude
and now in solitude has built her nest;
and in solitude her dear one alone guides her,
who also bears in solitude
the wound of love."

Commentary

2.   First the Bridegroom
praises the solitude of the soul
so much desired;
now she rests,
in peaceful solitude in the Beloved,
undisturbed by desire for satisfaction,
comfort, and the support of creatures.

Second, He says
that He is enamored of her
because of this desire for solitude.
He takes her in His arms,
He becomes her pastureland of all good things,
and He guides her spirit
to the high things of God.
And, as He says,
He not only guides her
but He guides her alone,
without any other means,
whether of angels, men, forms, or figures.
She now possesses
true liberty of spirit.

Theme: Peaceful solitude; liberty of spirit under the guidance of the Bridegroom.

1.   We now begin the final section of *The Spiritual Canticle*, written four years after the previous stanzas—a monologue of the Spouse, in a spirit and tone which is more tranquil, at peace, without a trace of the former anxiety. The calm assurance which comes from possession is much in evidence.

The Bridegroom has now led us into solitude; we are at peace with Him alone, wanting nothing more. We need no other light, no other guide. St. Thérèse had arrived at this state, and she says quite firmly, "Jesus alone is my guide." Normally we need the help and guidance of an experienced director; this is now not necessary. Directors should take note; there comes a time when they are dispensable. In fact, their task is to make themselves dispensable, and as soon as possible.

2.   What pleases the Beloved is our desire for solitude, "so much desired"; it is a desire for solitude "for the sake of the Beloved," not, be it noted, for its sake alone. This in itself is not meritorious or virtuous, and could be simply escapism. It is the solitude of pure detachment; now we can understand the insistence of the Saints that they live by love alone, without any other means, whether of angels, men, forms, or figures.

We find we no longer need the help which formerly in our spiritual lives seemed necessary—images, statues, particular prayer, formulas or exercises, a spiritual director; now we possess true liberty of spirit. With all this comes a true appreciation of rules, regulations, laws. These are seen in context; we realize that law follows life, not vice versa; but in no way is our respect for law diminished—quite the contrary. We have discovered the freedom of heart of the children of God, "the glorious liberty of the children of God" (Rom. 8:21). "Where the Lord's Spirit is, there is freedom" (2 Cor. 3:17). Not that we dispense altogether with spiritual direction— St. John of the Cross says elsewhere that "he who directs himself directs a fool"—but we no longer have the need, as before, for a director. We know that with God's help we are on a sure path.

3.   *"She lived in solitude"*:
        The turtle dove, the soul,
        formerly lived in solitude;
        until she finds Him,
        everything causes greater solitude.

4.   *"and now in solitude has built her nest"*:
        Formerly she practiced solitude in trial and anguish;
        now she has found
        the "nest" of complete refreshment and rest.
        "Truly the sparrow has found a house
        and the turtle dove a nest
        where she can nurture her young" (Ps. 83:4).

5.   *"and in solitude her dear one alone guides her"*:
        God guides, moves, and raises her to Divine things,
        elevating her intellect to Divine understanding,
        moving her will freely to Divine love,
        filling the memory with Divine knowledge,
        for the faculties are now emptied
        of all that is not God.
        Cf. Rom 8:14: "Moved by the Spirit of God."

6.   *"her dear one alone . . . who also bears"*:
        Having left all other means—
        angels or any other creatures—
        or natural ability or sense—
        the soul has now God alone
        communicating Himself
        without any intermediary.
        God alone is her guide.

7.   *"who also bears in solitude
        the wound of love"*:
        The Bridegroom also
        is wounded with love,
        having found in her
        the desire to live alone
        to all created things.

3–4. Paragraph 4 explains paragraph 3. Previously, by our own efforts, we tried to acquire solitude as a necessary means to union with God—at least "solitude of the heart," even in the midst of activities. It caused no little "trial and anguish"; it was not easy to be alone at first, and the opportunities for being alone, in any case, were few, and the need for solitude always caused a certain conflict and tension; nearly everyone striving for a more contemplative form of life finds this.

This seems to be part of God's plan to bring us to deeper detachment; He gives the desire for solitude, but He seldom indulges it! However, in this state of union, this kind of conflict ceases. There is now a solitude within, of the heart, which nothing really disturbs; the turtle dove has found a "nest of complete refreshment and peace."

5. "The faculties, intellect, will, memory, are now emptied of all that is not God." We live "divinely"; now we are "moved by the Spirit of God"; we resemble the Blessed Virgin, of whom St. John of the Cross said, "Such were the works and prayers of the most glorious Virgin Our Lady, who, being raised to this high estate from the beginning, had never the form of any creature imprinted in her soul, neither was moved by such, but was invariably guided by the Holy Spirit" (Asc.III.2).

6–7. The Beloved, too, like every lover who lives in a "world apart," once "wounded with love," guides us in the ways of love.

251

Introduction

1.   Lovers like to be alone.
       The presence of a stranger
       hinders their enjoyment
       of each other's company.
       Love is a union between two alone.
       The soul's only activity now
       is surrender to the delights
       of the intimate love of the Bridegroom.
       Compare Tobias, who, after much trial,
       spent all the rest of his days in joy.

2.   Isaias 58, 10–14: "Then your light
       will rise up in darkness . . ."

       "Let us rejoice, Beloved,
       and let us go forth to behold ourselves in your beauty
       to the mountain and to the hill,
       to where the pure water flows,
       and further let us enter deep into the thicket."

Commentary

3.   The bride asks for three signs:
       the joy and savor of love,
       to become like the Beloved,
       and to know the secrets of the Beloved.

4.   *"Let us rejoice, Beloved"*:
       Let us rejoice—
       not only in the sweetness of our union,
       which is habitual,
       but in the practice of love,
       the works directed to your service.

Theme: The soul's only activity—surrender. The beauty of God is savored and shared. She asks to share the secrets of the Beloved.

1. Two people who are in love desire above all to be alone. Conversation with others wearies them; St. Teresa refers often to this. Useless conversations become wearisome; we want to be alone with God, and our charity is taxed to the utmost.

    Note that in this stanza the Introduction seems to have no direct bearing on the rest of the commentary.

2. This paragraph is devoted to the "Advent" quotation from Isaias: ". . . then shall you be like a watered garden and like a fountain of waters, whose waters shall not fail . . . if you do not your own ways, and fulfill not your will, then shall you delight in the Lord, and I will lift you up above the high places of the earth, and I will pasture you upon the inheritance of Jacob." All of which St. John sees fulfilled and verified in this exalted state at which we have arrived; there is only one thing left now, he says: ". . . to enjoy Him perfectly in life eternal." It should be understood that the poem takes an important turn at this point; we are asking from now on till the end of the poem for the completion and culmination of all that we have experienced, by God's grace—nothing less than the "clear vision of God," the Beatific Vision.

3. Not only love, but to savor love; not only to become like the Beloved, but to know His secrets—the secrets of God!

4. If St. John did not constantly remind us, we might think that at this stage at least, the contemplative life would consist in being "alone with the Alone"; not so. The practice of love consists in "works in the service of the Beloved." The exercise of loving. "both interiorly and exteriorly," has this in view, namely, that "we should become more like the Beloved."

5.   *"and let us go forth*
       to behold ourselves in your beauty":
       Let us be so transformed in your beauty
       that we may be alike in beauty,
       both beholding ourselves in your beauty,
       since both of us
       are your beauty alone.
       May your beauty be my beauty,
       and my beauty, yours.

6.   *"To the mountain and to the hill"*:
       "The mountain" is essential knowledge of God,
       knowledge in the Divine Word.
       "The hill" is the wisdom of God
       in His creatures, works, and decrees;
       "Hill," a lower or lesser knowledge.

7.   So the soul makes two requests:
       to be transformed
       into the beauty of Divine Wisdom,
       the Word of God, and to be enlightened
       to the beauty of God's creatures.

5.   In the original text, St. John uses the word "beauty" (*hermosura*) twenty-three times, in as many lines. This theme of beauty is a whole study in St. John of the Cross. He was simply overwhelmed by the beauty of God and it comes through in all his works, especially in the poems. The extraordinary repetition in this passage can only be explained by the fact that the Saint in writing it was overcome by the thought that this very beauty of God becomes ours; the spouses, beholding each other, see each other's beauty. The consequences for us are amazing—that God should say to us, "All my things are Thine and Thy things mine" (Jn. 17:10). Cf. Stanza 6 and Stanza 11, notes 6–8.

Always, we are reminded, "Christ's by essence, ours by participation"; we are adopted sons, not natural sons. Lest we should forget that it is only in and through the Church and as "members of His Body, which is the Church" that all these graces come to us, St. John places the mystical experience of the Spiritual Marriage firmly within the context of the Church. It is not, and can never be, simply a private, individual experience. This would be to overlook the mysterious, mystical, but real identify between Christ and His mystical Body, the Church, and every member of it. Mysticism adds to the institutional and sacramental aspects of the Church, an enrichment which makes for fullness and completion, which will be realized when we, the Church, "share the beauty of the Spouse when we see God face to face."

6.   At this stage of Divine union, we can be content only with complete knowledge of God, both in himself and in His Creation.

7.   To speak of the Wisdom of God is to speak of the Divine quality which, in the Old Testament, was most readily associated with God himself; in the Wisdom books we find Wisdom personified, accompanying Yahweh in the work of Creation (Pr. 8:22–36), as a heavenly being reflecting the majesty and attributes of divinity (Wis. 7:24–8:1), and compared to the Divine Word throughout the Old Testament. Against this background, St. Paul, who was much influenced by the Book of Wisdom says, "Christ is the Wisdom of God" [1 Cor. 1:24]. Hence. St. John's words: " . . . the Divine Wisdom, the Word of God."

8.   Compare Canticle 4:6: "I shall go to the mountain of myrrh
      and to the hill of incense";
      the clear vision of God,
      and the knowledge of His creatures.

9.   *"to where the pure water flows"*:
      The "water" of knowledge and wisdom of Divine truth,
      her desire for this knowledge increasing
      in proportion to her love.

10.   *"and further let us enter deep into the thicket"*:
      "Thicket," because God's wisdom is so limitless,
      immense, as to be incomprehensible;
      the soul can always penetrate further
      into the mystery of the knowledge of God.

11.   Compare Ps. 18:10–12: "The judgements of the Lord
      are more to be desired
      than gold and precious stones,
      sweeter than honey and the honeycomb."
      "The soul judges it happiness for her to endure
      all the afflictions and trials
      of the world, even death
      to enter still further into her God."

12.   The "thicket" can also signify
      the sufferings of the soul,
      the trials and tribulations she endures
      as the means of entering the thicket
      of the delectable wisdom of God.
      Suffering brings with it
      knowledge of God from within,
      the purest and highest joy.
      "Deep into the thicket"—
      that is, into the agony of death (cf. Job 6:8–10).
      "May He who made me destroy me,
      let loose His hand
      and put an end to me,
      that in afflicting me with sorrow
      He might not spare me."

8.   The "clear vision of God" is always accompanied by an ever-increasing love and appreciation for creatures, and for all of God's Creation. In this sense, the mystics are the only "realists." Material things have a special meaning and sacredness in the light of the Incarnation and the Resurrection. So we ask for "the knowledge of His creatures" as well as knowledge of God himself.

9–11. As love increases, so does desire; we can never be satisfied in our search for a deeper knowledge of God; and we know that even in eternity we shall never sound the depths of God's wisdom and goodness. This is one of the joys of heaven—an eternal quest, in joy, of the Beloved. In this life, to attain this knowledge, we would endure all the trials and afflictions possible in order to have one moment of fruition of God, to "enter still further" into His loving wisdom and goodness.

12.   Perhaps we feel a certain disappointment or disillusionment on reading this paragraph. Even now, must there be suffering? Yes, says the Saint, and "the soul desires to enter, since suffering is most delectable and most profitable to her." It brings with it "the most intimate and purest knowledge"; but, he hastens to say, "the purest and loftiest joy which comes from having penetrated into the deepest knowledge." The well-known passage from *The Ascent*, Book II, chapter 7, contains the same thought regarding "spiritual persons who think any kind of reformation suffices," who become "enemies of the Cross of Christ." Here, "not content with any manner of suffering, we ask, 'Let us enter farther into the thicket,'" suffering even unto death if necessary. Cf. I.C. Mans. VII.3: The soul has "a great desire to suffer, allied to an extreme longing that the will of God be done . . . and a great peace of soul about suffering."

13.   If we could know that a soul
cannot reach the wisdom of the riches of God
without suffering;
and how the soul
with an authentic desire for Divine Wisdom
wants suffering!
Hence, St. Paul exhorts the Ephesians
not to grow weak in their tribulations,
to be strong, and rooted in charity,
in order to be filled
with the fullness of God (Eph. 3:13–19).
The gate of entry is the cross,
and it is narrow;
few desire to enter it,
while many desire
the delights of entering there.

13.   St. John proceeds: "The soul with an authentic desire for Divine Wisdom wants suffering!" It is the truth of the Paschal Mystery; only in the "passage" or "passing over" from death to life can we come to the glory of the Resurrection. St. Peter wanted only the glory, without the Cross, on Thabor; it was not to be. Although this is the message of Christ, "few desire to enter it, though many desire the delights of entering there." "There is no other way than the royal road of the holy Cross" (*The Imitation of Christ*).

1.   The first thing the soul desires in the next life
       upon coming to the vision of God
       is to know and enjoy
       the deep secrets and mysteries
       of the Incarnation.

       "And then we will go on
       to the high caverns in the rock
       which are so well concealed;
       there we shall enter
       and taste the fresh juice of the pomegranates."

Commentary

2.   Once the bride has entered further
       into the Spiritual Marriage,
       which will be the face-to-face vision
       of the glory of God in heaven,
       as well as union with Divine Wisdom,
       which is the Son of God,
       she will know the sublime mysteries
       of God and man.
       She will become engulfed,
       immersed in these mysteries,
       both bride and Bridegroom
       sharing the sweetness of this knowledge
       along with the discovery
       of the powers and attributes of God—
       His justice, mercy, wisdom, power, and charity.

Theme: Sharing the Bridegroom's knowledge of the mysteries of the Incarnation.

1. Throughout *The Spiritual Canticle*, St. John has made it clear that the culmination of God's gift to us in this life is that He allows us to "know and enjoy the deep secrets of the Incarnation." Faith in this profound mystery of the "Word made flesh and dwelling amongst us" is enlightened by a knowledge and understanding in faith of this mystery, which can only be a very special gift of God and comes only to those who enter into the Spiritual Marriage. This is a foretaste of what heaven really is; "this is life eternal, that they may know Thee, the one only true God, and Jesus Christ, whom Thou hast sent" (Jn. 17.3). Now we look forward to that time when, "set free," "seeing Christ face to face," we may reach the perfect understanding of these mysteries when faith gives way to vision—the Beatific Vision.

2. Not the least of the blessings of heaven is the mutual sharing of this knowledge "of these sublime mysteries of God and man." Both bride and Bridegroom 'seem to progress together in the "discovery of the powers and attributes of God." Then we shall know and understand what at present we accept in faith— the mysterious truth that God *is* justice, mercy, wisdom, power, love. Cf. St. Paul, Cor. 13:12; "Now I know in part, then I shall know as fully as I am known"; 1 John 3:2: "What we are to be in the future has not yet been revealed; all we know is, that when it is revealed we shall be like him, because we shall see him as he really is."

3.   *"And then we will go on*
    to the high caverns in the rock":
    The rock is Christ.
    The high caverns, the deep mysteries of God
    in the Hypostatic Union
    and God's union with men,
    along with the mystery
    of God's justice and mercy
    in judging and redeeming the human race—
    these are deep and impenetrable mysteries.

3.   "The high caverns in the rock; the rock is Christ" (1 Cor. 10:4).
The greatest mystery of all is the Hypostatic Union, God
becoming man. St. John's remarkable devotion to the Divine
Infant was not based on sentiment, but on his profound
understanding of the mystery of the Incarnation. It is not
surprising that we find the same emphasis in St. Teresa; in
her writings she is continually recalling us to the Sacred
Humanity of Christ. The person of Jesus was everything to St.
Thérèse of Lisieux, and it could well be that she drew inspiration
for the meditation and teaching on the merciful love of God
from passages such as this in *The Spiritual Canticle*. Most of
the quotations from St. John of the Cross in her writings are
from *The Spiritual Canticle*; she knew it thoroughly.

Along with the mystery of the Incarnation, we must consider
"God's justice and mercy in judging and redeeming the human
race." St. Thomas Aquinas tells us that each succeeding gift
of God to us—the revelation of the Trinity, the Incarnation,
the Blessed Eucharist—follows logically from the others. The
Eucharist was to be expected, in view of God's desire to give
himself totally to us.

4.   *"which are so well concealed"*:
        So well concealed,
        that no matter how much
        holy doctors and saintly souls
        have discovered of Christ
        there are always new riches to be found,
        for Christ is like a rich mine,
        always revealing new veins of wealth,
        inexhaustible.
        "In Christ dwells all the riches
        of wisdom and knowledge" (Col. 2:3).
        The soul cannot enter these caverns
        without having received
        many intellectual and sensible favors from God,
        and without having undergone
        much spiritual activity.
        These are inferior
        to the real gift of God,
        but serve as preparations
        for coming to this wisdom.
        God told Moses
        that He could not reveal His glory to him,
        but that He would show him
        all the good which can be revealed in this life,
        revealing to him
        the knowledge of the mysteries
        of the humanity of Christ.

5.   The soul, earnestly longing
        to enter these caverns of Christ,
        is invited to hide herself
        in the bosom of the Beloved:
        "Arise, make haste, my love,
        my beautiful one,
        and come into the clefts of the rock
        and into the cavern on the wall"
        (Cant. 2:13–14).

4.   Paragraph 4 should be read, reread, and meditated on. There
        is no end to the riches to be found in Christ; no matter how
        much theological knowledge we may have acquired, or what
        we may have enjoyed, the mysteries of Christ are inexhaustible.
        "In Christ dwells hidden all the treasures of wisdom and
        knowledge" (Col. 2:3). But only through much suffering, much
        effort, and only by a special gift of God can we sound the
        depths of the wisdom of God, "which is in Christ Jesus, Our
        Lord."

5.   In the previous paragraph, St. John suggests that the mysteries
        of the humanity of Christ were revealed to Moses. Whatever
        we may think of this interpretation, it is clear that the Saint
        regards the greatest grace of this time as that of "entering these
        caverns of Christ," "hiding itself in the bosom of the Beloved."

6.   *"there we shall enter"*:
        "We," because the Bridegroom
        is now always with her;
        in her knowledge
        of the predestination of the just
        and the foreknowledge of the damned,
        the soul is most sublimely transformed
        in the love of God.
        United with Christ,
        she thanks and loves the Father.

7.   *"and taste the fresh juice of the pomegranates"*:
        The pomegranate's many little seeds
        are held in a round shell;
        so God's attributes,
        mysteries, judgements, virtues,
        are sustained in God.
        Compare Canticle 5:14: "Your belly
        is of ivory set with sapphires"—
        that is, your wisdom is surrounded
        by these mysteries and judgements.
        Let it be remembered
        that each attribute of God is God himself.

6.   We do not say "we shall enter alone"; but "we shall enter"
      for "the soul does not work by itself without God." Mysteriously,
      we are enlightened as to the Divine judgement of the just and
      the wicked; the words used are "predestination of the just,"
      but foreknowledge (*"presciencia"*) of the "wicked," which
      could mean "foreknowledge of the fate of the wicked." This,
      in the context, seems most likely as this is the prerogative and
      power of God.

      Lest we should think that this is a seeming exaggeration, we
      must remember that it is precisely this Divine knowledge,
      presupposing foreknowledge, which is the gift of God in this
      state. A rather terrifying kind of gift, we may think, but remember
      that we are speaking of the next life, not this (cf. paragraph
      1). We should notice the frequency of the repetition of "in
      Christ" in these paragraphs, which is reminiscent of St. Paul's
      "in Christ" in the Epistle to the Ephesians, and elsewhere. The
      whole subject of his writings and teachings and the full force
      and meaning of St. Paul's use of "in Christ" can be understood
      in the context of St. John's insistence on Christ, and union
      with Christ, as the central, focal point of close union with God.

7.   St. John is trying to tell us that it is only through the knowledge
      revealed to us by God, of the mysteries of Redemption, that
      we can come to a knowledge of God himself. The pomegranate
      in his imagery represents some particular attribute of God, and
      the seeds represent "a great multitude of wondrous ordinances
      and admirable effects of God." By using this image, the Saint
      is attempting to convey the infinite variety of the mysteries and
      attributes of God, and what a tremendous grace it is for us
      to share in this infinity of God.

      It is not at all clear in what sense he uses the term "judgements
      of God," but the sense of his message is clear. And he goes
      on to enunciate the central point in our understanding of the
      attributes of God. It is also the most mysterious, since we cannot
      in any way visualize or conceptualize. Each attribute of God
      is God himself; God *is* love, He *is* wisdom, goodness, beauty,
      and so on. Apart from Scriptural revelation on this point, this
      follows from the very nature of God. Cf. Stanza 14 and Stanza
      15, notes 5–8. The second image, taken from the Song of Songs,
      is repetition of the same idea; but we might wish that St. John
      would confine himself to one image at a time!

8.   Just as from one pomegranate
there is one juice from many seeds,
so one fruition and delight of love,
the drink of the Holy Spirit,
overflows into the soul.
With tenderness of love
she at once offers this drink
to the Word, her Spouse,
as promised in the Canticle 8:2:
"There you will teach me
and I shall give you the drink of spiced wine
and of juice from my pomegranates."
Tasting it, He offers it to her,
and she in turn offers it to Him;
and they taste together.

8. Paragraph 8 speaks of the new wine from the crushing of the pomegranate seeds, the fruition of the sharing of God with us which must follow from this loving communication of this knowledge of Himself. A kind of inebriation follows, which St. John calls the "drink of the Holy Spirit," indicating that in this intimate experience of the Divinity, the Holy Spirit is the reason and cause of this union of love. Not only has He brought us to the "Word, our Spouse," but He shares intimately in this love relationship.

Introduction

1.   In the two preceding stanzas
       the song dealt
       with the transformation of the Bride
       into the created and uncreated wisdom of God,
       and into the beauty
       of the union of the Word with humanity.
       In this stanza she discusses two things,
       the manner in which she will taste
       the Divine juice of the pomegranate,
       and the glory she will give to her Bridegroom
       through her predestination.
       These are not really successive,
       but one glory.

"There you will show me
what my soul has been seeking.
And then you will give me,
you, my life, will give me there
what you gave me on that other day."

Commentary

2.   The soul now asks God
       to show her what she has longed for
       from the beginning—
       how to love Him
       as perfectly as He loves her.

Theme: The soul asks for a love as perfect as the Bridegroom's.

1. We should look back to Stanza 36, paragraph 7, to see what is meant by being transformed into the created and uncreated Wisdom of God. We asked for God's own understanding of His Creation, the lesser (created) wisdom and beauty contained in the mysterious works of God. Not only this; we asked to be transformed into the Word himself, wisdom itself, the "uncreated wisdom."

    Now, with the assurance that this extraordinary favor will indeed be given us, we speculate on how this will come about. And having done this, with a holy assurance, we proceed to remind the Bridegroom of the joy and the glory we shall give Him because of His gift to us; which St. John calls "our predestination." The word is used designedly; it is bound up with St. John's opinion that only those already confirmed in God's grace can reach the exalted state we are describing. Cf. Stanza 2, paragraph 3: "I think that this never happens without the soul being confirmed in grace"; and "being confirmed in grace" is nothing other than being "predestined" in a special way.

    Of course, we are all "predestined" by God for heaven in the sense that "God made us to know, love and serve Him, and to be happy with Him forever"; but having reached the Spiritual Marriage, we have already a foretaste of the Beatific Vision, though our certainty of salvation in this life is never absolute, or unqualified. There always remains the condition "if we are faithful."

2. Perhaps in this sentence we have the acme of desire in one who loves God, and it is always the desire of the true lover; perhaps also the sign of the true lover that he should not be outdone by the other in loving; we ask God to let us love Him "as perfectly as He loves us." Too daring a request? Not in the language of true love.

3. *"There you will show me*
    what my soul has been seeking":
    The soul wishes
    the clear transformation of glory,
    desiring, like every lover,
    equality of love,
    at the same time
    knowing that perfect consummation
    is impossible in this life.
    Then, "she will know
    as she is known by God" (1 Cor. 13:12).
    Her intellect will be that of God,
    her will His, her love His.
    The two wills are so united,
    while retaining their identity,
    as to be only one will
    and one love, God's.
    The strength of God's will
    which unites them
    is the Holy Spirit,
    who supplies what is lacking in her.
    So in the Spiritual Marriage
    the soul loves in some way
    through the Holy Spirit.

4. The soul states,
    not that God will give her His love
    —which He does—
    but that He will show her
    how to love Him
    as perfectly as He loves her,
    as though putting an instrument in her hand
    and showing her how to operate it
    in unison with him.
    Although in Spiritual Marriage
    there is not the perfection of heavenly love,
    there is nonetheless
    a living and totally ineffable semblance
    of that perfection.

3.   Now St. John clarifies his statement; we ask for what we know is impossible in this life, nevertheless we do ask. This means that we give expression to desires, and it is the desire which pleases God. Daniel was a "man of desires"; a seventeenth century poet, Thomas Crashaw, described St. Teresa as "thou undaunted daughter of desires." She herself regarded the desire for the love of God as already the accomplishment; the desire itself from God. The lover, then, desires "equality of love," knowing that in heaven this will be realized; "love equalizes."

St. John really gives us in this paragraph an insight into the meaning of heaven; we shall then "know as we are known by God." How this is brought about is explained; the Holy Spirit supplies for our natural defects, and what is impossible by nature becomes possible, and is really effected, by the grace of the Holy Spirit. Mary asked, "How can this be done?" And the Angel answered, "The Holy Spirit will come upon you." What was accomplished in Mary is to be done in us; "the two wills are so united as to be only one will, and one love, God's." The soul loves, "through the Holy Spirit." The soul can perform no acts, but it is the Spirit that moves it to perform them; so all its acts are divine—it is impelled and moved to them by God (cf. L.F.I, 4).

4.   This is not realized fully, even in the Spiritual Marriage, but, St. John says, "there is nonetheless a living and totally ineffable semblance of that perfection."

5.   *"And then you will give me,*
       you, my Life, will give me there
       what you gave me on that other day":
       Why, since essential glory lies
       in seeing God and not in loving,
       does the soul request,
       not essential glory, as of first importance,
       but love?
       First, because loving is giving,
       as knowing is receiving;
       so the soul in love
       thinks first of what she can give—
       of surrender to God.
       Second, the desire to see
       is included in the desire to love;
       one presupposes the other.

6.   *"what you gave me on that other day":*
       Means the day of God's eternity,
       when God destined the soul to glory.
       The "what" is the vision of God,
       which "No eye has seen, nor ear heard,
       nor has it entered into the heart of man . . ."
       (1 Cor. 2:9, cf. Is. 64:4).

5.   Perhaps the Saint deals with this point for the benefit of the
     theologians; he knows the true lover does not deal in fine
     distinctions, nor is he interested in the finer analysis of the
     process of loving; he simply loves. But if "essential glory" is
     in seeing God, the "Beatific Vision," why are we asking for
     love, not sight, or vision, of God? The Saint explains: loving
     is giving; seeing, or knowing, is receiving. After all, he says,
     you cannot have one without the other. Just as faith presupposes
     love, and is informed by it, although one is not the other, they
     must go together.

6.   We think of eternity as being in the future; not so says St. John
     of the Cross: the "day of eternity" is that in which God, from
     all eternity, predestined us for glory, actually determining the
     glory which He would give us. He gives it freely to us, freely
     without beginning, before He created us. Mysterious as it seems
     in the light of God's foreknowledge, we now can lay claim
     to that for which God had from all eternity predestined us.
     The Saint devotes many lines of the explanation to the word
     "what" ("*aquello*") in the poem, emphasizing the fact that no
     words can describe the joy that awaits us. He quotes from
     St. Paul: "Eye has not seen . . ." (1 Cor. 2:9; cf. Isaiah 64:4).

7.   Christ said to St. John in the Apocalypse:
"To him that overcomes
I will give to eat of the tree of life
which is in the paradise of my God,"
and "be faithful unto death
and I will give you a crown of life" (Ap. 2:10);
and "To him who overcomes
I will give a hidden manna
and a white stone,
and on the stone
a new name will be written
which no one knows
save him who receives it" (Apoc. 2:17);
and Apoc. 2:26: "he who overcomes
and keeps my commandments to the end,
to him will I give power
over the nations . . .
and I will give him the morning star";
and Apoc. 3:5: "He that overcomes
will be clothed in white garments,
and I will not cross his name
from the book of life.
And I will confess his name
before my Father."

7.   St. John draws heavily on the Apocalypse in order to give us some insight into the life of heaven awaiting us. But, as he says, "even after all this, much still remains unsaid." We note the repetition of the thought, "To him who overcomes," "Be faithful unto death . . ."

The nature of the reward can only be hinted at, though by means of striking imagery: "a crown of life," "hidden manna," "a new name," "power over nations," "the morning star," "clothed in white garments, his name will not be crossed from the book of life," and, most striking of all, "I will confess his name before my Father."

8.　　Apoc. 3:12: "And I will make him who overcomes
　　　a pillar in the temple of God,
　　　and he shall go out no more.
　　　And I will write upon him
　　　the name of my God . . .
　　　and also my new name."
　　　And "To him that overcomes
　　　I will give to sit with me on my throne,
　　　as I have also conquered
　　　and sat with my Father on His throne . . ."
　　　Yet all these expressions of grandeur
　　　do not explain the "what" of the verse.

9.　　The soul says
　　　that "what" God predestined for her from eternity
　　　He will give her
　　　on the day of her nuptials,
　　　loosed from the flesh,
　　　and gloriously transformed into Him.

8–9.   We should read this against the background of the Biblical notion of "name"; the tremendous significance of "writing on him the name of my God" points to a complete change of status, so that something in the person undergoes a radical and profound change; an elevation to the Godhead itself. The radical change or renewal of the person is effected; "I will write upon him . . . my new name."

We recall the great significance of Jesus' changing Simon's name to Peter; it implied and actually effected a complete change in the person of Peter, imparting to him qualities which naturally he lacked; Simon did become "the Rock" after Pentecost; strong, courageous and reliable, by the action of the Holy Spirit. Cf., in the Old Testament, the changing of the names of Abraham (Abram), Jacob (Israel) indicating both a new relationship with Yahweh and a new mission and the power to carry it out. Cf. also Isaias 62:2: Yahweh shows His redeeming love for Zion by conferring a new name. The choice of quotations from the Apocalypse and the Psalms reminds us that there is always a "mystical" dimension in the interpretation of texts which have become familiar to us from long usage, and which, taken literally, convey very little. Reading St. John of the Cross heightens our perception of this.

Introduction

1.   The soul says something
of what she will enjoy in the Beatific Vision,
explaining what she already experienced
of the "what."

"The breathing of the air,
the song of the sweet nightingale,
the grove and its living beauty,
in the serene night,
with a flame that consumes and gives no pain."

Commentary

2.   The "what" is described under five aspects:
it is the breath of the Holy Spirit
from God to her and from her to God;
it is rejoicing in the fruition of God;
it is the knowledge of creatures
and their orderly arrangement;
it is pure and clear contemplation
of the Divine essence;
it is the total transformation
in the immense love of God.

Theme: Looking forward to the Beatific Vision; breathing of the Holy Spirit; participation in God.

1–2. Already there is a foretaste of the Beatific Vision, but in this, the second-last stanza, we look forward to what will actually be experienced in the fullness of that glorious vision. Glancing down the list of five headings describing the *"aquello"* (which translates unsatisfactorily into English as "what"—cf. Stanza 38) we find it a complete résumé of the main themes already developed in *The Canticle*: the Holy Spirit, fruition in love, knowledge of creatures, loving contemplation in the night of faith, total transformation into God.

What surprises us is the prominence given to "knowledge of creatures," but this reminds us of the importance placed by St. John on finding God in Creation. The whole stanza is a welcome elaboration on each theme, and is invaluable for its insights into these five aspects of the contemplative life. Again, the concentric method of St. John is in evidence; we remember, too, that these last stanzas (35–40), written some four years later as an addendum to the original, deal even more profoundly with these themes as the Saint draws on his own ever-deepening experience of the intimacy of God.

3.   *"The breathing of the air"*:
Making her capable of breathing in God
the same breath of love that the Father
breathes in the Son, and the Son in the Father,
which is the Holy Spirit himself.
The tongue cannot describe this,
nor can the intellect grasp it.

4.   Cf. Gal. 4:6: "Since you are sons of God,
God sent the Spirit of His son into your hearts,
crying, 'Abba, Father!'"
This breathing from God to the soul
and the soul to God takes place quite frequently,
though not in the open and manifest degree
as in the next life.
This should not cause surprise
nor be thought impossible;
this breathing is through participation.
It is not incredible, therefore,
that she should understand, know, and love
in the Trinity, together with it,
as does the Trinity itself!
God accomplishes this in the soul
through communication and participation.
It is for this that God created her
in His image and likeness.

3.   In paragraphs 3–7 we have some of the Saint's most precious
        teaching on union with God, or "transforming union" (St. John
        never used this term, nor did St Teresa). We should reread
        paragraph 3 against the Scriptural notion of "breath," or "spirit":
        a divine, dynamic entity by which Yahweh accomplished His
        ends—as saving, as creating, the charismatic instrument of His
        power. In the New Testament, God revealed to us that the Spirit
        dwells in us and we in the Spirit (Rom. 8:9) in a Divine manner
        of existence communicated through Christ; so that the Spirit
        is the principle of life and activity proper to the Christian. He
        "reveals the deep things of God" (1 Cor. 2:10–16). He is the
        Spirit of faith (2 Cor. 2:4, 13), of hope (Gal. 5:5), of love; the
        "love of God is poured forth into the heart by the Spirit" (Gal.
        5:25); it is the Spirit which awakens love in the Christian (Cor.
        1:8).

        St. John initiates us into a tremendous mystery, speaking with
        the authority of one who knows from experience; as the Father
        breathes in the Son, and that breath of love is the Holy Spirit,
        we, in this high contemplative state of the Spiritual Marriage,
        are so closely united to God that, marvellous to relate, we
        become capable of breathing in God the same breath of love,
        the Holy Spirit. No wonder St. John says, "This is not to be
        described by mortal tongue, nor can human understanding,
        as such, have any conception of it."

4.   Lest we should think that the Saint is referring only to the Beatific
        Vision, he goes on to say, "This breathing . . . takes place quite
        frequently." It should not cause surprise; it is not impossible!
        We come to know, understand, and love in the Trinity, together
        with it, as does the Trinity itself. It is not incredible, for, as
        St. John says, "it is for this that God created us in His image
        and likeness." St. Teresa says, "We seldom consider what it
        means to be created in the image and likeness of God," and
        "It is a great shame not to know who we are in these terms
        (I.C. Mans. I.1).

5.   This is what Christ meant when He said,
        "Father, I desire that where I am
        those you have given me may also be with me,
        that they may see the glory you have given me" (Jn. 17:24)—
        that is,
        that they may perform in us
        the same work as I do by nature,
        "that is, breathe the Holy Spirit
        that they may be one
        as we are one, I in them and you in me;
        You have sent me
        and you love them as you have loved me"
        (Jn. 17:20–23). The Son does not ask
        that the Saints be one with Him
        essentially and naturally,
        as He is one with the Father,
        but through union of love.

6.   Souls, then, become truly gods by participation,
        as the Son does by nature.
        Compare 2 Pt. 1:2–5: "May grace and peace
        be accomplished and perfected in you
        in the knowledge of God
        and of Our Lord Jesus Christ;
        as all things of His Divine power
        which pertain to life and piety
        are given us through the knowledge of Him
        who called us with His own glory and power;
        by whom He has given us
        very great and precious promises
        that by these
        we may be made partakers
        of the Divine nature."

7.   How then can souls remain blind
        to such brilliant light,
        failing to discern
        the worthlessness of the worldly glory
        they are seeking?

5.   St. John, in interpreting the words of Jesus (Jn. 17:24), speaks
        with assurance which surprises us; it is the assurance of the
        mystic, and he says that the "work" which the Word performs
        in the Trinity by nature is the breathing of the Holy Spirit. "Being
        with Him," "seeing His glory" is, for us, to perform the same
        work—breathing the Holy Spirit. For Jesus said, ". . . that they
        may be one, as we are one, I in them and you in me." Have
        we not said to ourselves, at some time, "How can this be done?"
        It really sounds incredible; but with one luminous sentence
        the Saint explains; and this sentence is the key to understanding
        all that has been said regarding the nature of the union of
        the soul with God: ". . . not in the order of being, but in the
        order of love"! Here are the Saint's words: "It is not to be under-
        stood here that the Son means to say to the Father that the
        Saints are to be one in essence and nature, as are the Father
        and the Son; but rather that they may be so by union of love,
        as are the Father and the Son by unity of love."

6.   When the Saint, then, makes such extraordinary statements as
        "souls become truly gods by participation, equals of God and
        His companions," he is simply commenting on the remarkable
        passage quoted from St. Peter's First Epistle, regarding "the
        very great and precious promises" which have been given us.
        In his sublimest moments St. John of Cross never goes beyond
        the Scriptures; he always echoes the Gospel; he lived the Gospel.
        That is what the mystical life, contemplation, really means—
        living out the Gospel in its ultimate demands. Cf. Hans von
        Balthasar: "The highest flights of contemplation encompass
        regions no more remote than those attained in principle in
        the primary act of divine grace. Contemplation should be
        conceived Biblically" (*Prayer*).

7.   Paragraph 7 in the text is really a series of exclamations,
        expressing the Saint's disappointment, pain, incredulity that
        anyone who realizes these truths could be so unfortunate, so
        foolish, as to be blind to the truth, and deaf to God's call.
        "What are you doing? What is this wretched blindness?" he
        cries out. "You who were created for these wonderful things
        and called to enjoy them?"

8.   *"the song of the sweet nightingale"*:
The voice of both bride and Bridegroom
call to each other
in the new spring of their love;
"Arise, make haste, my love, my dove,
my beautiful one, and come;
for now the winter has passed,
the voice of the turtle dove
is heard in our land" (Cant. 2:10–12).

9.   "Your voice is sweet" (Cant. 2:14).
Because the soul praises God with God himself,
it is highly perfect and pleasing to Him.

10.   The soul now anticipates the delight
of the song she will sing in the next life,
that of the *"sweet nightingale."*

11.   *"the grove and its living beauty"*:
The grove is God, the living beauty:
that which the soul finds
not only in God
but in all the harmonious beauty of His Creation.

8–9.   The song of every true lover who has ever known the love
       of God, the sigh of the Beloved in the Canticle of Canticles:
       "Arise, my love, my dove, my beautiful one, and come." Bride
       and Bridegroom call lovingly to each other. Such perfect
       understanding exists between them; the voice of the bride is
       in some way the very voice of the Bridegroom, and is sweet
       with the praise of God himself, "highly perfect and pleasing
       to Him." It is noteworthy that the capacity to praise, to adore
       God in this way is the first fruits of the union of love. Hence
       the value we should place on every prayer of adoration. "[The
       soul]," says St. Teresa, "has no desire to exist except to add
       to God's honor and glory" (I.C. Mans. VII.3).

10.   Sweet as this song is, it is still not to be compared with that
       of the life to come; there we shall sing "like the nightingale."
       This theme of "a new song" runs throughout the Psalms and
       the Prophets (cf. Ps. 33:5, Is. 42:19).

11.   In Stanza 5, "grove" stood for the elements in God's Creation;
       now it means God himself, the living beauty in whom is all
       beauty—"beauty's self and beauty's giver." For the con-
       templative, everything in God's Creation is inseparable from
       God, and speaks of God. Compare the poetry of that great
       contemplative, Gerard Manley Hopkins, who in the "thisness"
       ("*haeceitas*") of things saw, felt, touched, and possessed God.

12.   *"in the serene night"*:
This night is the contemplation
in which the soul desires
to behold these things.
It is called night because of its obscurity.
On this account
contemplation is also termed mystical theology,
meaning the hidden or secret knowledge of God.
In contemplation God teaches the soul
very quietly and secretly,
without its knowing how,
without the sound of words,
and without the help
of any bodily or spiritual faculty,
in silence and quietude,
in darkness to all sensory and natural things.
It is sometimes called knowing and unknowing.
This knowledge is produced,
not as in natural knowledge—
in the agent intellect—
but in the passive intellect.
This receives only substantial knowledge,
divested of images
and without any active function
of the intellect.

13.   This knowledge, however sublime,
is still dark
when compared to the beatific knowledge
she asks for here.
The "serene" night
is the clear and serene vision of God in heaven.
Cf. Ps. 138:11: "the night
will be my illumination in my delights."

12.   This is, perhaps, the most comprehensive and instructive
       passage of St. John's teaching on contemplation. It is an effort
       on his part to state, clearly and succinctly, what he means
       by this mysterious thing "contemplation." It is "night"; in
       darkness, yet it is luminous; it is obscure, yet it is a knowledge
       of the deepest things of God—a knowledge which comes from
       God himself, "quietly, secretly, without the soul's knowing how."

       It is not to be confused with knowledge in the ordinary sense
       of that word, for in contemplation all natural means of knowing
       and understanding cease. It is at once "knowing, and un-
       knowing." Natural knowledge comes through images, concepts,
       ideas; this knowledge needs none of these intermediaries. The
       intellect simply does not function in the ordinary way; it simply
       receives passively ("in the passive intellect"); we understand,
       not knowing how. And if we could explain how we know and
       indeed, what we know, adequately, this would not be con-
       templation.

       Only by a special gift of God can any explanation be given
       (such as in the teaching of St. John). The Saint refers here
       to the "active and passive intellect," using the accepted
       scholastic terminology in describing the theory of knowledge.
       St. Thomas postulated the existence of an "agent intellect" in
       his theory of knowledge—that function of the mind which
       presents "forms, fancies, and apprehensions" to the passive
       intellect, thus giving birth, so to speak, to knowledge. In the
       contemplative knowledge of which St. John speaks, however,
       only the passive intellect is brought into play, receiving
       substantial knowledge directly, stripped of all images.

13.   It is not precisely this kind of "contemplative" knowledge of
       God which we are asking. It is nothing less that beatific
       knowledge, or that of the elect in heaven; the "serene" vision
       of God; unalloyed, perfect knowledge in the fullness of love.
       The word "serene" is used designedly of the "clear, beatific
       contemplation" of heaven. It is uninterrupted communion in
       serenity; eternal tranquillity in the vision of God.

14.   *"with a flame that consumes and gives no pain"*:
The flame is the Love of the Holy Spirit,
a consuming flame
that bring to completion or perfection.
Although God is a "consuming fire,"
the love spoken of gives no pain,
as is experienced in this life
in the transformation of love;
rather, God consummates and restores,
He does not destroy, as, in this life,
fire acts on coal.

15.   The soul asks
that the knowledge and communications of God
be given in a love which is consummated,
perfect and strong.

14.   St. John gives a special meaning to "consume." It means, he says, "to complete and perfect" ("*acabar y perfeccionar*"). Which explains St. Paul's use of the phrase "consuming fire" when applied to God—God who perfects, brings to completion, maturity. The fire, or flame, is the Holy Spirit; he "consummates and restores," gently, painlessly. A fire indeed, but never destructive. This is the first suggestion, in *The Canticle*, of the Holy Spirit as a "flame". This is, perhaps, the taking-off point for the Saint's further development of this theme: the Holy Spirit as the Living Flame of Love (his last work, *The Living Flame of Love*, was written in 1585).

15.   The Saint speaks of the "strongest and loftiest love" ("*fortisimo y altisimo amor*") needed, as God's gift, in order to love according to the greatness of her new knowledge in the vision of God. This is an important point, which he has made all along—that knowledge and love must go together, complementing and fulfilling each other.

"No one looked at it
nor did Aminadab appear;
the siege was still;
and the cavalry,
at the sight of the waters, descended."

Introduction and Commentary

1.   The soul mentions five blessings:
Her soul is detached
and withdrawn from all things;
the devil is conquered
and put to flight;
the passions are subjected;
the appetites are mortified;
the sensory part is reformed,
purified, and brought into conformity
with the spiritual.

2.   *"No one looked at it"*:
The soul is now detached, alone,
withdrawn from all created things,
both from above and below.
No longer can creatures disturb her
either by their sweetness or their misery.

3.   *"nor did Aminadab appear"*:
As in Canticle 6:11,
Aminadab is the devil.
Formerly he continually strove
with all the armaments and force he could use
to thwart the soul's entry
into the fort of interior recollection
with the Bridegroom.
But now, she is so strong in the virtues,
in the embrace of God,
that the devil does not dare to enter,
so afraid is he.

Theme: Perfect detachment achieved, the devil conquered; expectation of the Beatific Vision.

1. One looks, perhaps, for some sublime rapturous words on the blessed state finally attained. Instead this final verse and its commentary is very much "down to earth." We have noted the same thing in the final chapters of *The Interior Castle*. The "five blessings" listed deal with detachment and the purification of the passions and appetites, and the final victory over the devil and temptation. What was set out as a necessary condition for progress at the outset is now achieved; the result: perfect conformity of the sensory part with the spiritual.

    We are now, finally, "led by the Spirit." St. John says that now, finally, we set all these before the Beloved, as if to say, "All that you required of me has been done; now bring all things to their conclusion."

2. Detachment, from things "above and below"; and if this still needs explanation, it means that we have reached the point of not desiring even the spiritual goods or consolations which God does not desire for us. This is a reminder again that all these sublime gifts of God in this state may be given and experienced in great darkness, while all within the "interior castle" is at peace.

3. To the very end, the Saint refers to the Song of Songs. Aminadab, a name which does not seem to be patient of exact interpretation, St. John calls—in somewhat cavalier fashion—"the devil." It suffices for his meaning, as he wishes to emphasize the reality of the devil's action in the past, when he used every effort to prevent the entry into interior recollection, which St. John calls "a fort" that is impregnable. The devil cannot enter there, nor penetrate the citadel of faith. Strong as we are now in the virtues, the devil is helpless and, indeed, afraid.

4. *"the siege was still"*:
The "siege": the soul's passions and appetites,
threatening on all sides .
She knows that she cannot have the vision of God
until her four passions
are directed to God, and mortified.
She asks God for this.

5. *"And the cavalry,*
at the sight of the waters, descended":
The "cavalry": the bodily senses,
which are now so purified and spiritualized
that they have "sight of the waters,"
or share in and enjoy in their own way
in the spiritual grandeur of the soul.

6. The soul says
"at the sight of the waters":
Not *taste* of the waters, since the sensory part
has no capacity in this life,
or in the next,
for the essential tasting of spiritual goods.
The senses can, though,
through a certain spiritual ovearflow,
receive sensible refreshment
and delight from them.
In going down—"descended"—
the senses discontinue their natural operations
and are drawn to the spiritual recollection of the soul.

4.   The battle which rages within or around us, that of the struggle with our passions and inordinate desire, is called a "siege," and we ask that, once and for all, the battle will be stilled that we may enter upon the vision of God; for seeing God is impossible until this happens.

5.   The teaching has been stated clearly before, and indeed throughout the commentary: the bodily senses are so purified that they share in the spiritual joy and grandeur of the soul; in fact, they become in some way so "spiritualised" that perfect harmony exists between the "lower" and the "higher" natures. St. Paul complained about the "sinful principle" in himself; he found himself "doing the evil his will disapproved"; his "natural powers were at the disposition of sin" (cf. Romans 7:14–25). So it is with us all, but "the grace of God, through Our Lord Jesus Christ" can, and does set us free, as in the case of St. Paul. This is the freedom of which St. John of the Cross speaks.

6.   The "whole man" is now completely spiritualized in the way St. John has described; flesh and spirit no longer war against each other, and the spiritual joy of the higher faculties of intellect, memory, and will overflow into the senses, which "discontinue their natural operations." That this is possible in this life is stated in the following paragraph.

7.   The bride
        sets all this perfection and preparedness
        before her Beloved, the Son of God,
        desiring that He transfer her
        from the Spiritual Marriage
        to the glorious marriage of the Church Triumphant.
        May the most sweet Jesus,
        Bridegroom of faithful souls,
        be pleased to bring all who invoke His name
        to the glorious marriage.
        to Him be honor and glory,
        together with the Father and the Holy Spirit,
        in saecula saeculorum. AMEN.

7.   "All this perfection and preparedness are set before the Beloved" only that the Son of God, seeing what He has achieved in the soul, might take her to the celebration of the glorious marriage of heaven.

We have seen this in the lives of the Saints; while certain physical causes could be adduced for their death, there seems to be definite evidence that they quite simply died of love, and of desire for the Bridegroom. A little before her death, on receiving the Most Holy Sacrament, St. Teresa cried out, "My Lord and my Spouse! The longed-for hour has arrived; my Love, and my Lord, it is time we saw each other . . . time that my soul should rest in You whom I have so much desired."

With St. John of the Cross we will make this our prayer: "May the most sweet Jesus, Bridegroom of faithful souls, bring all who invoke His name to this glorious marriage."

AMEN

BIOGRAPHICAL NOTE
St. John of the Cross

St. John of the Cross was born in 1542 at Fontiveros, a small town about twenty miles from Avila, the birthplace of St. Teresa. His father, Gonzalo de Yepes, of a noble family, had been disinherited when he married a poor silk-weaver, Catalina Alvarez. Shortly after John's birth, his father died, and his mother sought the assistance of her late husband's relatives. They treated her unkindly and refused financial help; the poor widow moved to Arevalo with John and his elder brother, Francis. From there they moved to Medina, the great market center of all Spain, but Catalina's efforts to support the family by weaving brought little income and she was forced to place John in an orphanage, where he remained until the age of 17. He was unsuccessful in learning a trade, and finally the administrator of the local hospital, noting his charity for the poor and his diligence in collecting alms, offered him a post as a male nurse. He carried out his duties well. At this time he was admitted to attend classes at the Jesuit college nearby, and without detriment to his work in the hospital he studied at night and successfully completed a four-year course of studies.

He was now 21, and his thoughts turned to the religious life. He asked for admittance to the Carmelite Order and was accepted, spending a year in the monastery before proceeding to Salamanca University, where he spent three years, being ordained as a Carmelite priest in 1567, at the age of 25. He returned to Medina del Campo, and his mother, brother, and sister-in-law assisted at his first Mass.

A few months later, he was introduced to St. Teresa, who in 1562 had founded the first house of the Discalced Carmelite Reform for nuns at St. Joseph's, Avila. She had received permission from the General of the Carmelite Order to found similar houses of the strict observance of the Primitive Rule of Carmel among the Carmelite friars. As it happened, John too was seeking a stricter form of life, and hoped to join the Carthusians. St. Teresa persuaded him to join the Reform, and he agreed, on the condition that the first foundation be made without delay. In November of that year he returned to the University of Salamanca, where he took a year's course in theology. He then returned to Medina del Campo, and accompanied St. Teresa to Valladolid, where a foundation of the Discalced Nuns had been made. He remained for some months, learning the ways and customs of the nuns with the help of St. Teresa.

After returning to Avila, he proceeded to Duruelo, a small, out-of-the-way village some thirty miles away. He was accompanied by a lay-brother, and they prepared the small farmhouse there, a gift from a gentleman from Avila, with a view to making the first Discalced

Carmelite foundation for friars of the Order. The house, poor as it was, was officially declared a Discalced Carmelite Monastery by the Father Provincial on the First Sunday of Advent, 1568. The first Community, of five members, lived there very austerely and with fruitful apostolate to the local people for a year and a half, after which they moved to a more spacious residence in Pastrana, a hundred miles distant. From Pastrana, a third foundation was made at Alcala, an important university city, with St. John of the Cross as first Superior. After one year, a request came from St. Teresa for John of the Cross to act as spiritual director to the Convent of the Incarnation at Avila, where Teresa, against her wishes, had been appointed Prioress.

A fruitful period of spiritual direction followed, and a valuable association with St. Teresa for two years. He accompanied her to Segovia, then on his return took up his duties as confessor. During this time, misunderstandings arose with the Fathers of the Carmelite Order whom John had left to enter the Reform. John was imprisoned at Medina del Campo; he was regarded as a disobedient religious, and there was not a little resentment over the success of the Reform. It is impossible for us to assess the real situation or to make a judgement regarding the motives of the people concerned. John of the Cross, freed at the intervention of the Papal Nuncio, in December 1576, was shortly afterwards carried off by force to the Carmelite priory at Toledo and imprisoned there, in a small, dark cell, enduring great suffering, until on August 16 of the following year he escaped. During those nine months he composed thirty-one stanzas of *The Spiritual Canticle*.

Following the meeting of the Discalced superiors at Almodovar in 1578 he was sent to the monastery of the Discalced Fathers in El Calvario, Andalusia, southern Spain. During this time he wrote the prose commentaries for *The Ascent of Mount Carmel* and *The Spiritual Canticle*. Except for short periods he was to remain in Andalusia for the rest of his life.

There followed appointments to the monasteries of Baeza, as Rector of the College, and Los Martires, Granada, as Prior of the house and Third Definitor. In November of 1581 he met St. Teresa for the last time, in Avila; she died in October of the following year. From 1582 to 1588 he was mainly at Granada, with occasional visits to the Carmelite convent at Beas. During this time he wrote the last stanzas of *The Spiritual Canticle*; *The Living Flame of Love* and other poems; the commentary on *The Spiritual Canticle* (Second Redaction); and the commentary on *The Living Flame of Love*. It seems that he wrote nothing of importance in the last five years of his life.

He became Vicar-Provincial of Andalusia and made five new foundations. Re-elected Prior of Granada in 1587, he was chosen to attend the first Chapter-General of the Reform in Madrid, and was elected First Definitor and Consultor. In the same year he became

Prior of Segovia, Castile, the central home of the Reform. He was re-elected First Definitor at the extra-ordinary General Chapter at Madrid, but he fell into disfavor with the General of the Discalced, Fr. Nicholas Doria. He was deprived of his offices, and the decision was taken, but afterwards revoked, to send him to Mexico. Instead he was sent to the isolated monastery of La Penuela, in Andalusia. His health was failing, and he went to Ubeda for medical aid, but ten weeks later he died, after much suffering, at midnight on Saturday, the eve of the Feast of the Immaculate Conception, 1591. His body was laid to rest in Segovia.

John was beatified by Clement X in 1675, canonized by Benedict XIII in 1736, and declared Doctor of the Universal Church by Pius XI in 1926.